THE BOYS' BOOK
OF ADVENTURE

Written by Steve Martin
Illustrated by Simon Ecob

Edited by Hannah Cohen
Designed by Zoe Quayle

THE BOYS' BOOK OF ADVENTURE

Buster Books

DISCLAIMER

The publisher and author disclaim, as far as is legally permissible, all liability for accidents, injuries or loss that may occur as a result of the information or instructions given in this book.

This book was first published as *The Boys' Book of Adventure* in hardback in Great Britain in 2010 by Buster Books, an imprint of Michael O'Mara Books Limited, 9 Lion Yard, Tremadoc Road, London SW4 7NQ

This paperback edition was first published in 2010 by Buster Books,

9 Lion Yard, Tremadoc Road, London SW4 7NQ

www.mombooks.com/busterbooks

Text and illustrations copyright © Buster Books 2010
Cover design by Angie Allison (from an original design by www.blacksheep-uk.com)
Cover image by Paul Moran.

A CIP catalogue record for this book is available from the British Library.

ISBN: 978-1-907151-41-5

2 4 6 8 10 9 7 5 3 1

Printed and bound in July 2010 by Clays Limited, St Ives plc, Popson Street, Bungay, Suffolk, NR35 1ED, UK.

Papers used by Michael O'Mara Books are natural, recyclable products made from wood grown in sustainable forests. The manufacturing processes conform to the environmental regulations of the country of origin.

CONTENTS

SAFE ADVENTURES

The hints and tips in this book are intended for practice purposes only. A good adventurer should always keep his wits about him. Keep in mind that some ideas in this book are intended purely to help you imagine what it might be like to join an expedition to escape the curse of a pharaoh or to cross a rope bridge to safety. Under no circumstances should you ever attempt any exercise that would put yourself or others in any danger in real life.

You should, at all times, make yourself aware of, and obey, all laws, regulations and local by-laws, and respect all rights, including the rights of property owners. Always respect other people's privacy and remember to ask a responsible adult for assistance and take their advice whenever necessary.

Above all, remember to exercise good common sense and to take all necessary safety precautions when preparing to attempt any project, particularly when using heat or sharp objects. That said, it is fun to learn new skills that may one day prove useful on a real-life adventure!

Are you ready to face the challenge?

HOW TO READ AN ANCIENT MAP

Your adventures could take you anywhere in the world –
through dense jungle, across vast oceans or deadly deserts.
Wherever you go, you will need to be able to follow maps to
help you find your way.

If you ever discover an ancient treasure map inside an old
sea captain's chest, make sure you check the back for notes.

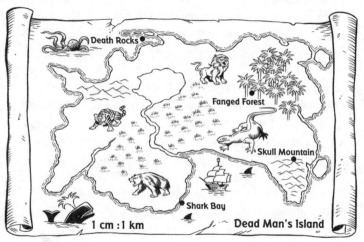

On the back of the map above someone has scribbled the
following instructions:

Land at Shark Bay. Walk 3 km north, keeping watch for the
quicksand that can drag you to your doom.

Turn east and walk 3 km, avoiding the savage beasts.

Walk south through the land of the fierce head-hunter tribe
for 2 km. Dig in this spot and you will be rich.

8

MAP-READING RULES

To find where the treasure is hidden, you will need a pencil, a ruler and these rules:

- If there isn't an arrow telling you which direction is north, it is usually safe to assume that the top of a map is north. The right-hand side is east, the bottom is south and the left-hand side is west.

- Maps usually have a scale. At the bottom of the map opposite you will see it says 1 cm : 1 km. This means that 1 centimetre on the map equals 1 kilometre in the real world.

WHERE IS THE TREASURE?

Follow the steps below to find where the treasure is hidden.

1. Place your ruler so that zero is at Shark Bay and the ruler points upwards (in the direction of north). Put a pencil mark at the 3 cm point.

2. You now have to walk 3 km east, so place zero where you made the mark and hold the ruler so it points to the right. Put a pencil mark at the 3 cm point.

3. The last direction tells you to head south, so your ruler needs to point downwards. Place zero at your latest pencil mark and measure 2 cm down the page.

4. Mark an 'X' where you think the treasure is. Turn this book upside down to see if you have found the correct spot.

Answer. The treasure is buried on Skull Mountain.

Now all you have to do is get past the quicksand, wild beasts and fierce warriors ... good luck.

HOW TO DIVE FOR PEARLS

Every adventurer knows that a pocket full of pearls will help pay for expeditions in an emergency. You've travelled to a town called Toba, on the east coast of Japan, to go diving for a very special treasure that lies 30 metres below the surface – oyster shells containing precious pearls.

The ancient tradition of 'free diving' (diving without breathing apparatus) is very dangerous and requires great skill because divers have to hold their breath for long periods of time. The method has almost entirely been replaced by scuba divers using the latest diving equipment ... except in Toba.

Keen to witness this dying art, you hitch a ride with a boat that is going free diving for pearls. Suddenly, people wearing nose clips leap overboard. Once on the sea bed, they scoop oyster shells into bags that hang from their necks, then speed back to the surface.

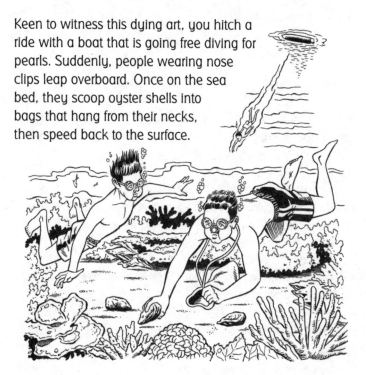

About 90 seconds later, the divers reappear gulping mouthfuls of fresh air. Back on the boat, each diver quickly opens the hard outer shells of their oysters with a sharp knife. Most shells are opened and cast aside empty. Eventually, there is a cheer as one of the divers opens his hand to reveal a gleaming white ball no more than two centimetres wide – a precious pearl.

PEARL-DIVING PRACTICE

Pearl divers are only able to dive to great depths after many years' training. You can practise diving for pearls in a swimming pool with this diving game to play with a group of friends.

1. Find six different types of coin – each coin will be a 'pearl' that you and your friends will dive for.

2. Throw the pearls into the pool so that they are spaced out.

3. Before you dive, decide on the order in which each pearl should be collected.

4. Using a stopwatch (or the clock on the pool wall), take it in turns to time how long each diver takes to collect the pearls in the correct order. The winner is the person who collects them in the fastest time.

Adventurous tip. Wear goggles and a nose clip like the real pearl divers to help your search for underwater pearls.

WARNING. Diving can be dangerous, so always have an adult present in case anyone gets into difficulty. Ask permission from the owner of the pool before you play the pearl-diving game. After you have finished playing, remove all the coins from the pool.

HOW TO CLIMB A ROPE TO SAFETY

Rope climbing is a skill that may one day save your life. Imagine … you can hear the howling of a pack of wolves in the distance. You are running as fast as you can, your breath making clouds of steam in the freezing night air as you struggle through the thick snow.

In this harsh winter, food is scarce and the wolves are starving. They've picked up your scent. Eventually, you fall face down and lie exhausted, listening to the barking of the hungry beasts.

You need to think fast. Looking up, you see a tall, strong branch high above your head. If you could just reach it and get off the ground you could save yourself from becoming dog food! Just in time, you remember you packed a rope in your backpack …

Read on to find out how to set up a safety rope that you can climb up to get out of danger.

You will need:
- a length of rope roughly 3 m long
- a strong, healthy tree • a stick

1. Tie knots in the rope, about 30 cm apart.

2. Tie one end of the rope to a stick (the stick acts as a weight to help throw the rope over the branch) and throw it over the strongest branch of your chosen tree.

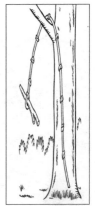

WARNING. Ask an adult to check the branch won't break when you put your weight on it.

3. Reach up and grab the end of the rope with the stick tied to it. Untie the stick and throw it away.

4. Tie a loop in one end of the rope and thread the other end of the rope through it. Pull tightly on the threaded end of the rope so that the loop reaches the branch. Your rope is now ready to climb.

5. To climb up the rope, bend your knees and wrap them around the rope. Rest your feet on the bottom knot. Now raise your hands up to the next knot and pull your body up. Lift your legs up until your feet reach the next knot. Repeat this until you reach the top.

6. To climb down the rope, use the knots to work your way down slowly. If you slide down too quickly, the rope could burn your hands – painful!

HOW TO BE A MASTER OF DRAGONS

Up until the beginning of the twentieth century, people living in Europe didn't know whether dragons were living creatures or if they only existed in myths and legends.

In 1910, however, a Dutch explorer named J.K.H. Van Steyn travelled to the Indonesian island of Komodo and discovered dragons roaming free. The photos he took on his island adventure proved to the world that dragons do exist.

DANGEROUS DRAGONS

Komodo dragons are the largest lizards on Earth. They can run up to 20 kilometres per hour, climb high trees, swim, dive to great depths and smell prey from several kilometres away. They have sharp claws, 60 sharp teeth and a deadly bite. They feed on birds, mammals and occasionally even humans ...

Perhaps the only person who could take on a ferocious Komodo dragon in unarmed combat and survive would be a master of the greatest of all martial arts – 'kung fu'. Students of this ancient art spend a long time practising the correct stances before moving on to learn how to fight a real opponent. The kung-fu move named the 'Dragon Stance' puts you in the perfect position to attack, defend and move quickly. This is because each part of this move copies the way a reptile, such as a Komodo dragon, moves and strikes at his prey.

MASTER THE KUNG-FU DRAGON STANCE

1. Step forward with your right leg, keeping most of your weight on your left leg. Bend both your knees.

In this position your legs are ready to spring into action to kick an opponent.

2. Stretch your right arm out and point your hand upwards in front of your face.

Position your hand so that you can see your opponent between your thumb and index finger.

3. Bend your left arm at the elbow and raise it so that it is slightly lower than your right arm. Keep your arms relaxed at all times, so that you can move them quickly to strike at an opponent.

This position allows your arms to move as fluidly as a dragon's powerful tail.

Practice makes perfect. One kung-fu master made his students stand on a horse cart in the Dragon Stance while he drove fast over bumpy roads to help build up the strength in their legs! Practising these moves regularly will help you build up strength in your legs and give you a powerful kick.

HOW TO SOLVE THE RIDDLE OF THE SPHINX

You're crossing the mountains and valleys of ancient Greece in the heat of a Mediterranean summer, heading for the city of Thebes. Hot, tired and dirty, you are suddenly confronted by a fearsome, winged beast – the legendary riddle-talking Sphinx.

You may have heard of a giant, stone statue called the Sphinx that guards the Great Pyramid in Egypt, but the original Sphinx lived in Greece. You find yourself staring into the eyes of a young woman, whose head is attached to a lion's muscular body. Two large feathered wings spread out menacingly on either side of her body.

The Sphinx stands blocking your path. Legend has it, she sets a challenge to all travellers who want to pass. They must answer the beast's riddle or be eaten alive. No one has ever answered her question correctly, which means no one has survived the Sphinx. Sure enough, she stares, her fearsome eyes burning into you, and asks:

'Tell me, what animal walks on four legs in the morning, two legs at midday and three legs in the evening?'

You sit and think. Surely no animal has different numbers of legs at morning, midday and night? Unless ... what if by morning, midday and evening, she means the beginning of life, when a baby crawls on all fours; the middle of life, when a man walks on two legs; and old age, when a man walks with a stick?

'Man!' you cry. 'The answer is a man.'

Despite the heat, your blood turns cold as the Sphinx lets out a roar and devours herself, allowing you safe passage into Thebes.

BE READY FOR RIDDLES

You must be prepared to solve all kinds of puzzles on your adventures. Why not take it in turns with a friend to set each other a riddle to solve? Below are some to start you off:

What goes around the world but stays in a corner? **Answer.** A stamp.

What gets bigger the more you take away? **Answer.** A hole.

What gets wetter the more it dries? **Answer.** A towel.

What goes up and down without moving? **Answer.** Stairs.

HOW TO BE A STORM CHASER

'Tornado warning! Stay in your homes and move into the basement!' blasts through the radio speakers. Ignoring the warnings, you're in a van in the Midwest of America, speeding towards the storm. You are a storm chaser and chasing powerful tornadoes and huge storms is part of your job.

Storm chasers risk their lives to learn more about a dangerous weather phenomenon called a tornado – a funnel of spinning air. Taking pictures and recording wind speeds as the tornado forms, your team drives full speed towards the storm.

The storm began over the ocean and moved slowly towards the American coast. Like a living beast, it fed on the energy of the warm Caribbean Sea, gathering power as it travelled. Spinning anti clockwise, the winds formed and gathered speed … 170 kilometres per hour … 200 kilometres per hour.

A STORM CHASER'S GUIDE

Experienced storm chasers stick to these guidelines to make sure they follow a tornado and live to tell the tale.

- Monitor weather reports carefully. This way you will know when a storm is coming and get there in time.

- Travel in a team. You need a driver, someone to take pictures and measurements, and someone based at a weather centre to tell you if the storm is changing direction.

- Know the area. Have a map and mark the roads that are safe to use around the path of the storm. You don't want to find yourself down a dead end with a tornado chasing you.

- Be aware of tornado danger signs. Before a tornado hits, the wind may die down and the air may become very still. Beware of clear skies on the edge of storms as this is often where tornadoes form.

- If you're chasing a tornado in a city, make sure your driver sticks to the speed limit and your team doesn't cause an accident.

WARNING. Tornadoes are unpredictable and extremely dangerous. Never chase a storm unless you are with a team of experts.

STORMY SCIENCE

Tornadoes occur when the winds blowing above a thunderstorm move more quickly than the air lower down. This causes the air to spin. A spinning funnel forms, which sucks up air from below. This funnel grows until it is long enough to reach the ground, where it causes terrible destruction.

You can see a tornado spin in your own home simply by using coloured water instead of air. Here's how you do it:

You will need:
- two large, clear plastic bottles (empty) • duct tape
- food colouring • water

1. Fill one bottle two-thirds full with water.

2. Add a couple of drops of food colouring to the water in the bottle.

3. Ask someone to hold the second bottle on top of the bottle filled with water (so that the tops of each bottle meet), while you tape them together tightly with the duct tape.

4. Now turn the bottles up the other way, so that the bottle with the water in it is on top.

5. As the water begins to run into the bottom bottle, swirl the top bottle round and round in a circle. The spinning water moving into the bottle below is now moving faster than the water around it. This creates the tornado effect.

HOW TO FIND YOUR WAY IN A MAZE

According to Greek legend, the Minotaur was a savage creature with a human body and the head of a bull. It caused such terror on the island of Crete in Greece, that King Minos had a huge Labyrinth (which means maze) built around the beast to trap it. Every year, seven young men and women were sent into the Labyrinth as a gift for the Minotaur to eat.

One year, a young man called Theseus decided to travel to the Labyrinth to defeat the Minotaur and end the killings. No one had ever escaped from it alive. When Ariadne, the King's daughter, fell in love with Theseus, she said she would help him if he promised to marry her. Theseus agreed to her request, and Ariadne then handed him a ball of thread.

Before Theseus entered the Labyrinth, he tied the end of the thread to the entrance and let it unwind as he found his way through and killed the sleeping Minotaur. Following the thread back, he found the entrance and escaped the Labyrinth.

A-MAZE-ING SOLUTIONS

If you ever need to find your way in a maze, you could use Theseus' trick to help you. If you don't have any thread handy, here are some more maze-solving tricks to try.

- As you enter the maze, mark arrows on the floor using chalk, or stones – follow these back to the entrance.

- If you go down a dead end, walk back to where you turned into it. Draw a line in the ground across the path so you know not to go down it again.

- Below is a plan of one of the most famous mazes in the world, Hampton Court Palace Maze, in London. Thousands of people have spent hours trying to find their way to the centre and back out again surrounded by high hedges.

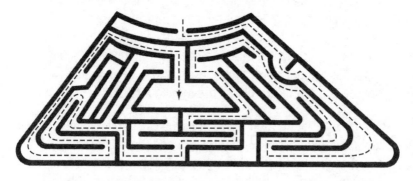

The solution is simple, however, and can be used to help you find your way through many mazes. By keeping your right hand touching the hedge at all times as you walk, you will get to the centre and back again. However, this route will take you down a few dead ends. If your adventures take you to this maze, take a copy of the solution above and find the centre without going down any dead ends.

DESIGN YOUR OWN MAZE

If you think you can design a more complicated maze than the one at Hampton Court Palace, you will need a sheet of large-squared graph paper, a pencil and an eraser.

1. Draw a square as large as possible on the graph paper. This is the border of your maze.

2. Erase two breaks in the edge of the square to create the entrance and the exit for the maze.

3. Use the lines on the graph paper to help you draw a path from the entrance to the exit. The graph-paper lines are the walls or hedges of your path. Remember to add lots of twists and turns as you go.

4. Make false paths which branch off from the main path. (Create breaks in the main path by rubbing out where you need to.)

All the false trails should finish in dead ends. Your maze should now look similar to the one here.

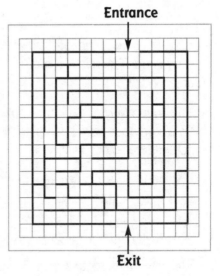

Entrance

Exit

5. Make photocopies of your maze – challenge your friends to find their way through it. Time each player's attempt. The player that does it in the fastest time, wins.

HOW TO REPAIR A SPACECRAFT

Space adventures are quite literally out of this world. If you do get fired off planet Earth, however, you'll need to be able to fix anything that goes wrong with your spacecraft ... after all, there are no garages in space! Read on to learn how to survive in space when your spacecraft breaks.

SPACECRAFT SURVIVAL

• Always wear a spacesuit. It protects you against the extreme temperatures of outer space (temperatures can range between 135°C to minus 82°C), from flying rocks that may collide with you, and it provides you with oxygen so you can breathe. A spacesuit costs over £12 million, but it is essential kit for all astronauts.

• Switch on your helmet camera so that what you see is relayed back to 'mission control' – your helpful team based back on Earth.

• To carry out repairs on your spacecraft, climb outside and switch on your helmet lamp so that you can see in the darkness of outer space.

• Fitted to your suit is a long thick line that is attached to your spacecraft. This line provides you with oxygen and allows you to communicate with mission control. They will be watching and instructing you on how to fix the damage.

• Locate the damaged area. To do this, astronauts use a gas canister to make sure they float in the right direction. To move forwards, fire the gas in the opposite direction – backwards. The force of the gas will push you forward.

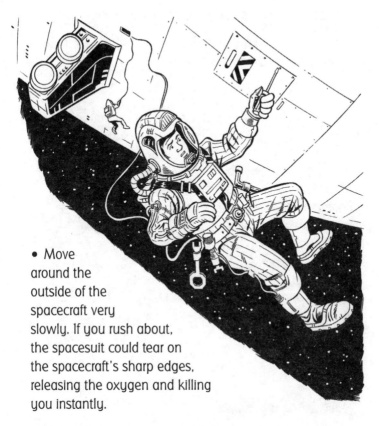

• Move around the outside of the spacecraft very slowly. If you rush about, the spacesuit could tear on the spacecraft's sharp edges, releasing the oxygen and killing you instantly.

• Use tools, secured to a tool belt around your waist, to fix the damage. Tools will float off into space if they are not attached to a tool belt.

• Space tools are specially made so that they can be used by astronauts wearing thick gloves. You can practise your spacecraft repair skills at home by trying to fix your bike wearing thick oven gloves.

Once you have fixed your spacecraft you are ready to continue on your space adventure. Mission accomplished.

MAKE AN IN-JEAN-IUS TOOL BELT

Follow these steps to make your own tool belt in which you can carry around essential equipment on your adventures.

You will need:

• a belt • an old pair of jeans you have grown out of • scissors
• tools (these could include a hammer, pliers, a torch, etc.)

1. Cut from the waistband down around one of the back pockets of your jeans. Leave a 3 cm gap around the edges of the pocket. Keep two belt loop holes at the top of the pocket.

2. Cut out one of the front pockets in the same way.

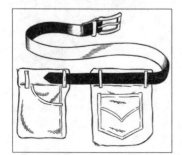

3. Thread the belt through each of the belt loops on the pockets.

4. Wrap the tool belt around your waist and fill the pockets with tools. You are now ready to fix anything with your tools handy.

HOW TO CRACK A SYMBOLIC LANGUAGE

Over two hundred years ago, French soldiers and geographers were digging in the heat of the Egyptian sun, when one of the sweating, exhausted soldiers suddenly stopped as his spade hit rock. Slowly he pulled a large, black stone out of the earth. The soldiers quickly noticed that this wasn't just any old stone. It was covered in strange markings.

They didn't know it at the time, but they had just discovered one of the greatest treasures of all time, far greater in value than gold or diamonds. This rock was the Rosetta Stone. On it were a set of symbols that no one knew how to interpret …

THE SYMBOLS EXPLAINED

The strange markings on the stone were symbols that were used in ancient Egyptian writing called 'hieroglyphs'. Among the symbols inscribed on the stone were an eye, a river reed and a basket. Hieroglyphic writing died out in Egypt after the fourth century and, shortly afterwards, so did the knowledge of how to interpret these mysterious symbols.

The Rosetta Stone was so valuable because it contained not just a set of hieroglyphs, but underneath them was the same text written in ancient Greek. Many years after the Rosetta Stone was discovered, scholars worked out how to use the stone as a 'key' to translate the hieroglyphs. From then on, scholars were able to translate other hieroglyphic words.

THE KEY TO A SYMBOLIC LANGUAGE

If you want to be able to send and translate messages using secret symbols, then you need to create a key, too.
Here's how:

1. Draw a grid that has 26 columns and two rows in it.

2. Write the letters of the alphabet along the top row.

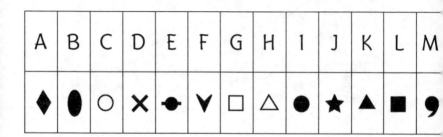

3. Draw symbols in each box under each letter of the alphabet. (You can use the same symbols as shown in the grid along the bottom of these pages or make up your own.) This is your key.

4. Write your friends a secret message using the symbols instead of letters to make the words you need.

5. Make enough copies of the key for each friend who needs to read and write the messages. When you receive a message, use your key to decode it.

CAN YOU CRACK IT?

Using the key below, can you work out what words the following symbols are spelling?

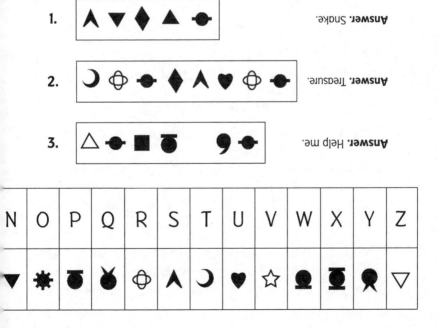

1.   **Answer: Snake.**

2.   **Answer: Treasure.**

3.   **Answer: Help me.**

N	O	P	Q	R	S	T	U	V	W	X	Y	Z

HOW TO BUST A GHOST

A true adventurer is brave and fearless, but there are some adventures that are so scary, they will send chills down your spine. Dealing with ghosts is right at the top of that list (if you believe in them). While most ghosts mean you no harm, it's understandable that you don't want to be sharing your space with a spook.

If you want to bust a ghost, always carry the following equipment, which will help you detect a spooky presence:

- A torch – in case the lights don't work.

- A thermometer – a sudden drop in temperature could be a sign of a ghost.

- A camera – if you see a ghost, take a picture for evidence.

- A mobile phone – to record strange bumps in the night.

CHECKING FOR GHOSTS

To check if you are being haunted by a ghost, try these tricks.

- Hold a piece of string in your right hand, with your arm stretched out in front of you. Loudly ask the ghost to give you a sign that it's nearby. If the string quivers, it may be your ghost showing you its presence.

- Choose a fixed point and stare at it for 30 seconds. Relax your eyes, but keep looking at the fixed point. If you see a shadowy shape in the corner of your eye, chances are you have a ghost.

GHOSTBUSTING MOVES

Once you are sure you are being haunted, try these ancient ghostbusting tactics to get rid of your ghost for good.

• Walk to the centre of each room in your house, and in a loud, kind voice, say, 'It's time for you to move on, this is not the place for you.' Repeat this five times in each room.

• Before you go to bed, decide which pair of shoes you will wear the next day. Put them at the end of your bed, and point one shoe in one direction and the other in the opposite direction. This is supposed to confuse a ghost and make it leave you alone.

• Sprinkle some grains of rice on the kitchen floor before you go to bed. The spook will not be able to stop itself counting each grain. Having to do this every night for a week will give it such a headache that it will leave for good. Don't forget to clean up every single rice grain as soon as you get up in the morning, or you'll have something even worse than a ghost to deal with – an angry mum.

HOW TO JOIN A BAND OF GORILLAS

If you're suddenly confronted by a huge, hairy, grunting creature, you could say, 'Good morning, Dad.' Or, if you happen to be trekking in the rainforests of Africa, you're more likely to have just met your first gorilla. Don't panic – gorillas make great friends if you know how to hang out with them.

Gorillas live in groups (also called 'bands') of between 6 and 30. A young male weighs 180 kilograms on average, and can be up to 1.8 metres tall when standing upright. Gorillas only attack when they feel threatened or afraid. Read on to learn if a gorilla is threatening you, or if it wants you to join its group and make friends for life.

AGGRESSIVE SIGNALS

- Showing its teeth doesn't mean a gorilla is smiling, it means, 'I'm threatening you.'

- Chest beating means, 'I'm angry and ready for a fight.'

- Looking straight into your eyes is a gorilla's way of telling you it is cross.

- Moving part of its body in your direction means, 'Go away.'

- Walking stiffly on all fours with straight arms means, 'I'm the boss and don't you forget it!'

- A gorilla will scream, grunt, bark and roar when it is really mad at you. If this happens, slowly back away. Wait until the gorilla has calmed down before going near it again.

FRIENDLY SIGNALS

If you don't annoy a gorilla, it will eventually get used to you and may start displaying more friendly signals.

- Making a high-pitched barking sound is a sign of curiosity. The gorilla wants you to come closer.

- When a gorilla extends its palm towards you, it means, 'Come here.'

- If a gorilla strokes your arm gently, it is saying it likes you.

- If the gorilla starts picking fleas out of your hair, you've made a new best friend.

GROUP TACTICS

If you're lucky enough to be accepted into a band of gorillas, here's how to spend your day living like one.

- Gorillas spend nearly half their day resting and half their day walking about finding food. They can travel up to 1,800 metres each day.

- Mountain gorillas are vegetarian, and fill up on leaves, stalks and shoots.

- As the sun goes down, gorillas like nothing better than bending soft trees and branches to make a cosy bed for the night.

WARNING. When you find yourself picking fleas out of your fellow gorillas' fur, you've stayed too long. Say your goodbyes and get back to your human friends.

HOW TO MAKE A SWIFT EXIT

Breaking into the crime boss's headquarters was meant to be impossible. However, as the head of the Secret Service said, if anybody could get in, it was you – the country's top agent.

You've avoided the dogs, dodged the guards, slipped by the electronic beams, cracked the combination of the safe, and removed the computer disk which contains enough information to send a gang of villains to prison for a long time.

As you wipe the sweat from your brow and slip the disk into your pocket, a piercing siren screams out and red lights flash.

You panic as you see a steel shutter sliding down to trap you in the room. If you don't move quickly, it's all over.

Running as though your life depends on it towards the shutter, you see it moving closer to the ground. You have been warned there may be acid that could burn your skin on the floor, so you can't drop to the floor and crawl through. Time is running out ... there's only one thing to do – the limbo dance.

You spread your feet wide, fling your arms out to the sides to give you balance and arch your back underneath the closing shutter. You straighten up on the other side, just as the shutter hits the ground with a clang. You've made it!

LIMBO FOR YOUR LIFE

Whether or not you're ever in a situation where you need to limbo dance to freedom, why not practise this life-saving skill by holding a limbo competition with your friends?

You will need:

• three or more friends • two bamboo canes (at least 1 m long) • a tape measure • a pen

1. On one cane, mark a point 60 cm from one end using your pen. Measure 10 cm sections from that point until you reach 1 m, making a mark each time. This is your measuring cane.

2. Ask two friends to hold the other cane at each end, around 1 m high, parallel to the ground. (Use your measuring cane as a guide.)

3. Take it in turns to limbo under the cane. To do this, spread your legs shoulder-width apart and stretch your arms out on either side of your body. Take small steps forwards towards the cane, bending your knees and leaning backwards as you move. Don't lean back too far – you will lose your balance and fall over. If a player's body touches the cane, or their hands touch the ground, they are out.

4. Lower the cane by 10 cm so that it is now 90 cm off the ground – in line with the mark on your measuring cane. Players must now try to limbo under it again.

5. Continue lowering the cane by 10 cm, making it harder to limbo underneath it. The player that can limbo the lowest, wins.

HOW TO FIND JURASSIC FOSSILS

The old Tyrannosaurus Rex lay down, his eyes closing as his life slowly drained away. The fight with the younger, stronger dinosaur had been too much and, this time, he knew his wounds wouldn't heal.

Millions of years passed. The jungle became farmland and then a village which, by the 21st century, had been washed away by the sea. Long forgotten, the poor dinosaur's old bones lay under the sand, their soft insides slowly turning into stone.

Until, one day, an adventurer notices an oddly shaped stone on the beach. Digging down deeper into the sand, he sees more and more strange stones. After 60 million years, the fossilized bones of the T-Rex have been found.

FOSSIL-HUNTER HINTS

Imagine finding an animal that has lain undiscovered since the Jurassic period – a time millions of years ago when dinosaurs walked the Earth. The remains of these creatures, whose flesh has long since disappeared, but whose bones have been preserved, are called fossils.

Follow this fossil-hunting guide to kick off your own discoveries.

What to take. Fossil hunters need to prepare a fossil-hunting kit. This should include a small hammer and a chisel to crack open rocks which you suspect contain fossils or to carefully extract a fossil from a rock; protective glasses to protect your eyes from flying rock chippings; a magnifying glass to identify tiny fossils; a fossil guidebook and a notebook to record your findings.

Where to go. Fossils are often found in places where there has been erosion (where rock has worn away), such as the bottom of cliffs. Water washes fossils out of the ground, so beaches, riverbanks and streams are also good places to search. Part of the English south coast (from East Devon to Dorset) is called the Jurassic Coast because of all the fossils that have been found there.

What to do with a find. If you find an interesting fossil, report it to your local museum. The museum staff may be able to give you more information about your discovery.

WARNING. If you are fossil hunting near the bottom of cliffs watch out for loose rocks falling above your head. On the beach, be wary of the changing tide. Never go fossil hunting without an adult.

FANTASTIC FOSSIL FINDS

Below are some fossil finds to look out for. The pictures on the right show how these creatures looked during the Jurassic period, and the pictures on the left show what they look like today as fossils.

AMMONITES

Ammonites were related to creatures such as octopus, squid and cuttlefish. They lived in the sea from 240 to 65 million years ago. They became extinct at the same time as the dinosaurs.

TRILOBITES

Trilobites were small creatures that lived on the sea floor. If you find one, it could be up to 560 million years old, and even the youngest will be 250 million years old.

ECHINOIDS

These are also known as sea urchins. They first appeared 450 million years ago. Unlike many creatures that lived during the Jurassic period, they didn't become extinct and are still found today.

HOW TO SWIM WITH DOLPHINS

Imagine swimming lazily in a warm, blue ocean while your boat rocks gently nearby. Suddenly, there is a shout from the boat's captain and you turn to find a great water creature swimming towards you at over 50 kilometres per hour. You freeze in fear at the sight of this beast as it raises its head out of the water to reveal ... the beautiful, smiling face of a dolphin.

Dolphins are intelligent, playful animals who generally like human company, although experts advise people not to go out looking for them. This is because wild dolphins can be dangerous. However, if you happen to meet a dolphin on your adventures, here are some dolphin-friendly facts you should know to make sure you make the most of a truly unforgettable experience.

DOLPHIN-FRIENDLY FACTS

Strong swimmers. You'll have to swim fast to keep up with a dolphin. In the wild, dolphins spend most of their time underwater and often travel over 60 kilometres a day.

Dolphin etiquette. Dolphins usually give humans a warm welcome because they are friendly creatures, so let the dolphins come to you. Never swim up to a wild dolphin – it might be in a bad mood.

Don't touch. A dolphin's skin is very sensitive and easily damaged, so avoid touching it. Dolphins can also catch diseases from human contact, so avoid swimming too close.

Pod games. Don't panic if a dolphin swims very close to another dolphin or to you – this is a sign of friendship. Dolphins live in groups called 'pods' and like to play games with each other. Favourite games include playing chase and tossing seaweed to each other.

Whistling words. Dolphins communicate by whistling. Each dolphin has a unique whistle so other members of the pod know who is calling. Other whistles have special meanings. For example, there is a whistle that means, 'Help!'

Clicking clues. If a dolphin wants to find you, it will, by making strange, clicking noises. The clicking is called 'echolocation'. The dolphins listen out for clicks that are bounced back from different objects – they can find an object no bigger than a pea from 100 metres away.

WARNING. If you want to swim with dolphins, you will need to take an organized tour. Do plenty of research beforehand to make sure the organization you go with is kind to dolphins.

HOW TO CHARM A SNAKE IN THE STREETS OF NEW DELHI

You have come to the end of an exciting adventure in the bustling Indian city of New Delhi. Wandering around a local market, you're hunting for presents to bring back for friends.

An old, bearded man is sitting cross-legged in the busy market-place with a wicker basket in front of him. He spots you and beckons you to come and sit with him. He hands you his flute, explaining that it has been carved from a vegetable called a gourd. The man tells you that in the basket is a vicious cobra that can kill a man with a single bite. Offering you the flute, he asks you to make some music for the snake.

You don't want this killer snake to be deprived of its music for one second, so you quickly cover the flute holes with your fingers and blow. Suddenly, the snake pops its head up from the basket. As you play, the snake begins to dance, swaying with the music.

The old man is a snake charmer and he learnt the craft from his father. Snakes are seen as sacred creatures in India, and the ability to hypnotize them and make them dance gives the country's snake charmers a mystical air.

SNAKE-CHARMING SECRETS

Lowering his voice, so as not to let his secrets out in front of the crowd that has gathered to watch, the snake charmer explains that the snake is not actually dancing to the music you're playing. In fact, snakes are practically deaf, and it responds to the shape and the movement of the flute as you're playing, rather than the music itself.

Your heart seems to stop as the old man leans forward and strokes the deadly reptile. Finally, he tells you to put the flute down and replaces the lid on the basket. There is a loud cheer and the crowd throws coins for the snake charmer.

Adventurous tip. Although snake charming provides income for people practising this ancient tradition, it is actually illegal in many of India's large cities.

You are an adventurer who likes to keep within the law, so give the man back his flute, and thank him for teaching you this new skill, before moving on to your next adventure.

HOW TO WRITE A HEROIC SAGA

In the past, heroes used to pay poets to write wonderful poems about the brave deeds they performed on their adventures.

These poems are called 'heroic sagas' and the poets who composed them could make even ordinary events seem amazing. If you want to write a successful heroic saga to describe one of your adventures, you need to follow these rules:

- Each pair of lines in your poem should rhyme.

- Turn ordinary objects into something ancient and grand by using words from the past, such as 'chariot' instead of car, or 'quest' instead of 'journey'.

- Use words such as 'loyal', 'bold' and 'intrepid' to describe your heroes – this will make the saga sound more heroic.

Anything can be made into a heroic saga if you try – even a trip to the supermarket … here's how.

THE SAGA OF THE SUPERMARKET POTATOES

Most sagas are about journeys, treasure or fair ladies:

> HE BRAVELY SET OFF IN HIS CHARIOT OF GOLD,
> DRIVEN BY HIS SERVANT, A CHARIOTEER BOLD.
> HIS QUEST WAS TO WIN FINE TREASURE,
> TO BRING THE FAIR LADY PLEASURE.

(This means you and your dad went out in your yellow car to buy potatoes for Mum.)

Make objects sound as impressive as possible:

> ARRIVING AT THE WONDROUS GATE,
> HE WAS READY TO MEET HIS FATE.
> THOUGH FRIGHTENED, HE DID HIS BEST TO MASK IT,
> AND BRAVELY GRABBED A SHOPPING BASKET.

(This means you went into the supermarket.)

Make your adventure sound more dangerous than it was:

> THOUGH HIS LIFE WAS IN DANGER,
> HE COURAGEOUSLY DID RISK IT,
> AS HE SEARCHED AMONG TOOTHPASTE,
> KETCHUP AND BISCUIT.
> THROUGH AISLE AFTER AISLE HE FOUGHT HIS FOES,
> UNTIL HE FOUND THE PRECIOUS POTATOES.

Whenever possible, make yourself sound great:

> HE FEARED NOT THE DARKEST CAVE OR HIGHEST HILL,
> FEROCIOUS DRAGON OR CHECKOUT TILL,
> TO HIS QUEST HE REMAINED LOYAL AND TRUE,
> AND STOOD TALL AND PROUD IN THE CHECKOUT QUEUE!

HOW TO ESCAPE THE CLUTCHES OF A BOA CONSTRICTOR

If you happen to meet a boa constrictor on an adventure, the good news is that these snakes are not venomous.

The bad news is that these reptiles can be over 4 metres long and over 30 kilograms in weight. They use their strong, powerful bodies to wrap themselves around their prey and suffocate it until it dies. They then open their huge jaws and enjoy a tasty feast. Read on to learn how to avoid becoming a snake's snack.

BE BOA-AWARE

Where they live. Boas live in the tropical regions of Central and South America. Although they live on dry land in hollow trees and logs, you may find one as you wade through rivers, as boas are very good swimmers.

Feeding habits. A constrictor will eat anything it can catch and swallow, including birds, monkeys and even pigs. A boa only wraps itself around something it intends to eat. It does not think of humans as food because they are too big for it to swallow, so it is very rare that a boa will attempt to eat you.

Sense of smell. A boa will only wrap itself around you if it smells another animal's scent on you and becomes confused. To avoid being mistaken for something a boa could eat, always wash your hands thoroughly after making a ham sandwich for your lunch in the jungle.

Boa bites. The mouth of a constrictor is filled with tiny, hooked teeth which it uses to hold its prey down. If a boa is frightened it will defend itself by biting you. This is painful, but not fatal.

Stay still. If you do stumble over a boa while out in the jungle, and it decides to attack you, don't struggle – this will only make it squeeze tighter. Shout to someone else in your group to pour some vinegar into its mouth as this might make it release you. It this fails, grab your pocket knife and cut off its head.

HOW TO DRESS A WOUND

Unfortunately, there aren't many adventurers who don't get injured at some point. Usually, these injuries are no more than small cuts caused by clambering over ancient ruins or struggling through dense jungle.

Small wounds needn't be a problem, as long as you are prepared and know how to dress them properly. 'Dressing a wound' means applying a protective covering to the wound to stop any infection developing inside it. Here's how to do it:

ESSENTIAL FIRST-AID KIT

You can't dress a wound without a first-aid kit. Below are the essential items every adventurer should carry in his first-aid kit – they can mean the difference between life and death.

You will need:
- a clean cloth • fresh drinking water
- antiseptic cream • sticking plasters

The smallest wound can become very dangerous indeed if it becomes infected, so the most important thing to do is clean it. Follow these steps immediately.

1. If blood is still dripping out of the wound, press a piece of clean cloth gently against the wound. Applying some pressure should soon stop the bleeding.

2. Once the bleeding has stopped, pour some drinking water over it so that any little bits of dirt are washed away. Dab the wound gently with the clean cloth to dry it.

3. After washing and drying the wound, stop it from getting infected by rubbing a small blob of antiseptic cream all over it.

4. Now you need to dress the wound to keep the dirt out. The easiest way to do this is to use a sticking plaster. Peel the paper off the back and carefully lay the padded part of the plaster over the open skin.

5. Change the plaster whenever it gets dirty or wet. Each time you change the plaster, clean the wound thoroughly.

6. Check the wound regularly. If there is swelling or pus oozing out of it, if it continues to hurt, or if it doesn't appear to be healing, it may be infected and you should see a doctor as soon as possible.

WARNING. When dressing a wound, you should always get an adult to look at it first.

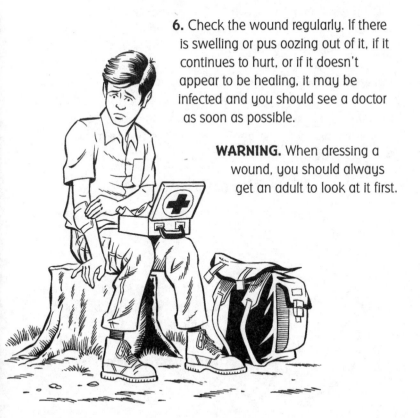

HOW TO MAKE A KEY DISAPPEAR

You are standing in the bank queue waiting to get to your safety-deposit box. Inside the deposit box is an ancient treasure map you found in an old sea captain's chest. You've researched and planned your treasure-hunting trip … all you need is the map.

Suddenly you hear shouting and look up. The bank is being robbed and one of the robbers is looking right at you! The robber has seen you anxiously holding the key which will open your safety-deposit box. He slowly walks towards you. Your fingers close tightly round the key. If the robbers get this key, they will have the map to the treasure!

You freeze in fear as the robber points at you and shouts to the other robbers that you have the key. One of the gang is guarding the door, so you can't run. Suddenly, you have an idea. You fight back panic and concentrate. This is going to be the most important magic trick you've ever carried out in your life …

ABRACADABRA!

Follow these steps to learn how to make a key vanish in the nick of time.

1. Hold the key in your left hand between your thumb and index finger. Your hand should be palm upwards with your thumb and finger pointing upwards.

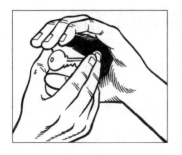

2. Put your right hand over the key and close your hand in a fist.

3. Just before you close your right hand over the key, let the key drop down from your thumb and finger and land in the palm of your left hand.

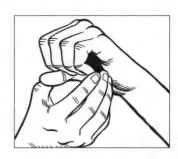

4. The robbers will think the key is in your right hand and will watch it carefully. While they do, slip the key from your left hand into your pocket. Open out your left hand to show the robbers that the key is not in this hand.

5. With your right hand, pretend to throw the key out of the window. The robbers will hopefully run outside and start looking for it. While they do, you can make your escape.

Adventurous tip. Practise this trick on your friends so you are ready to perform it perfectly in an emergency.

HOW TO TRAIN A FALCON

A falcon is a bird of prey, which means it hunts other animals for food. Throughout history, humans have trained birds of prey to catch food, such as smaller birds and rabbits, for dinner.

Falconry (the skill of flying trained birds), however, is also an ancient sport. One of the most thrilling sights is watching a huge bird fly down at incredible speed and land on its trainer's gloved hand – but there are some rules to remember:

• Never attempt to train a bird of prey without an experienced falcon trainer to assist you.

• Wear a falconer's glove – a thick leather glove which the bird can land on without hurting you.

• Wear dark clothing during training so that you don't frighten the falcon.

BIRD-TRAINING TACTICS

Follow these steps to teach a falcon to fly at your command.

1. 'Manning' is the process of getting the falcon used to you so that it will be ready to train to receive meat from your hand. First, put a small hood over the falcon's head – this will keep it calm and relaxed.

2. Tie a leash to the D-shaped ring on your glove. Thread the leash through a swivel (a metal joint) that is attached to leather straps (called 'jesses').

Attach the jesses to rings on the bird's legs. Place the falcon on your glove and remove its hood. Feed it raw meat until it becomes used to sitting on your glove without its hood on.

3. Put the falcon on a perch so that it can hop back to your glove to get a reward of meat. Once the bird is returning to your gloved hand, put its hood back on and take it outside.

4. Tie a 30-metre-long leash (called a 'creance') to one of the rings on the falcon's legs. Tie the other end of this leash to your glove, and untie the jesses from your glove. Place the bird on a perch and remove its hood.

5. Show the falcon a 'lure' – this is a leather pad attached to a cord with some meat on it. Throw the lure on the ground in front of the falcon – it should fly down to eat the meat on the lure. Put some more meat on your glove and it should now jump back across to the glove. Your bird is ready to fly free.

6. The first time you fly a bird free, it is a good idea to attach an electronic tracking device to make sure you can find it if it flies off. Remove the creance, then swing the lure in a wide circle above your head. As the falcon flies at the lure, jerk the lure away so that the falcon has to turn and chase the lure again. Regularly swinging a lure for the falcon will help keep it fit and healthy.

7. To return the falcon to your gloved hand, place a piece of meat on your glove and call to it. It should hop on and then you can tie its jesses back on to your glove to take it home.

HOW TO EMBARK UPON A MYTHICAL QUEST

There are many stories told about the legendary King Arthur, the noble warrior who helped save Britain from an invading tribe called the Saxons. As legend has it, Arthur had brave, loyal knights who worked for him. There are many tales that tell of the heroic adventures of his knights and the battles they fought in, but none fire the imagination as much as the 'quest' (which means search).

Knights were sent on many quests because it was the search itself that taught them how to be great knights. The journey was often seen as more challenging, fun and much more important than the prize they were looking for.

ARE YOU READY TO FACE THE CHALLENGE?

If you want to face the challenge of a search, why not organize a quest with a friend? Take it in turns to set each other a quest so that you both get to go on a journey.

You will need:

- a pen • six pieces of paper • sticky tape
- a prize (remember, it is the quest itself that's fun, so the prize doesn't need to be much – a bag of sweets will do)
- a friend who wants to set out on a knightly quest

You are going to leave a trail of clues leading to the prize that you will have hidden. On knightly quests, each clue must rhyme. On the opposite page are some clues you could set for your fellow knight. Give him the first clue and wish him luck.

Clue one. To discover where this quest goes,
Go and ask a beautiful rose.

(Hide clue two in the rose bushes in the garden or the park.)

Clue two. To solve the quest, use your wits,
Look under where a cyclist sits.

(Tape clue three underneath a bicycle seat.)

Clue three. To find the clue and learn your fate,
You need to open the magical gate.

(Tape clue four to the back of the park or garden gate.)

Clue four. A confusing clue is what you've got,
It's not in the kitchen, but it is in a pot.

(Hide clue five in a flower pot.)

Clue five. You're getting close, you're nearly there,
So have a rest and sit on the chair.

(Tape the final clue to the bottom of a chair.)

Final clue. Quest on brave knight and don't get tense,
You won't need to fight, but you may need to fence.

The final clue leads to the prize. Tape some sweets (or your chosen prize) to the garden/park fence to reward your fellow knight for understanding the clues and completing the quest.

HOW TO CROSS A ROPE BRIDGE

Faced with a fast-flowing stream while trekking on an adventure through the jungle, how will you make sure your team of adventurers and all the equipment make it to the other side without being swept away by the current?

As long as you've brought that most essential piece of adventurer's equipment – your trusty ropes – you can make a bridge that everyone can cross safely. Read on to learn how.

(If you're not planning on going on a jungle adventure soon, why not practise making your rope bridge at home between two strong trees?)

You will need:

- two long, strong ropes • thick fabric (offcuts from an old carpet or mat is ideal) • two trees, roughly 4 m apart • a tape measure

1. If you are on a jungle adventure, find a point along the stream where there are two strong trees on either side.

2. Measure 50 cm up from the base of the tree trunk, on the side of the stream that you are on. Tie some thick fabric around the tree at this point – this will protect the bark of the tree when you tie the rope to it.

3. Measure 1.5 m up the tree (above the wrapped fabric) and tie some more thick fabric around the tree here.

4. Now you need to secure the ropes to the tree. To do this, tie one end of rope around the bottom of the tree, at the point where you have tied the fabric, using a knot called a clove hitch. Follow the steps below to learn how to do this:

HOW TO TIE A CLOVE HITCH KNOT

5. Wrap the rope once around the tree trunk, crossing one end of the rope (A) over the other rope end (B).

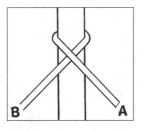

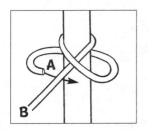

6. Wrap end A around the tree trunk again, making a second turn, and thread it under rope B, as shown.

7. Thread rope A under the second turn. Pull the rope through and tighten.

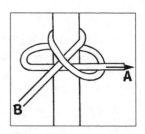

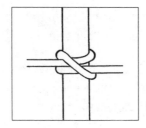

Pull on the ropes as hard as you can to make sure you have tied the knot correctly. This rope is for walking on.

8. Now you need to tie the end of the second rope over the fabric that is higher up the tree. Repeat steps **5** to **7** to secure this end to the tree. This rope will be for holding on to while you are crossing the rope bridge.

9. Gather the ends of both ropes in large loops. Wade carefully across the stream to the other side, unwinding the ropes as you go.

WARNING. Never wade through water that is deeper than your calf – strong currents may knock you off your feet.

10. Once you have successfully crossed the stream, tie the ends of each rope to the tree on this side of the stream, by repeating steps **2** to **8**.

Adventurous tip. It is very important the ropes are tied so they are not too slack. If the bottom rope is slack, it could dip into the stream when you stand on it. If the top rope is slack, it could cause you to tip over and fall into the stream.

CROSSING A ROPE BRIDGE

• Stand on the bottom rope, holding the top rope, and shuffle sideways across the bridge.

• If you have baggage to get across the stream, tie it to the top rope with a loop and pull it along to the other side.

• Only ever cross a rope bridge one person at a time – if the rope breaks, you and your baggage will get very wet.

HOW TO HAGGLE IN A SOUK

Hundreds of voices cry out in an unfamiliar language. The air is perfumed with exotic fragrances, and market stalls are piled high with brightly coloured cloth, ornaments and spices. This huge Moroccan 'souk' (which means market in Arabic) is unlike any shopping trip you have ever been on.

Stopping at a stall, you spy a coffee pot that would make a wonderful present for your grandparents. You pick it up and take a closer look.

'40 dollars, my friend! For you, only 40 dollars!' the stallholder is shouting at you.

'I don't have 40 dollars,' you reply.

'No problem! For you, 35 dollars!'

You stare at the pot, shrug, and put it down.

'No, thanks, that's too much.'

'30 dollars then. I can give it to you for 30 dollars.'

'No, thank you,' you say, hoping he'll drop the price again.

'30 dollars is my lowest price, my friend.'

Shaking your head, you start to walk away from the stall.

'Okay! Okay! 25 dollars. That is my final price. 25 dollars.'

You turn around and say, 'Okay, I'll give you 15 dollars.'

'20,' says the stallholder.

'Deal!' you shout and shake hands with the man.

The man raises his eyes to the sky and laughs. You have just haggled the stallholder down to a good price – well done!

HAGGLING KNOW-HOW

Get the price you want to pay when buying presents in a market with this haggling know-how.

Act disinterested. If you see something you like, stroll over to the stall and look at some other items before picking up the one you want. If the stallholder thinks you really want something, they will offer it to you for a higher price.

Meet in the middle. A good rule of thumb when haggling is to offer half the price that you think the item is worth. This way you can settle for the number in the middle.

Enjoy the haggle. If a stallholder has enjoyed haggling with you, he will most likely settle on a price you are happy to pay. Smile and make him laugh, and you'll not only get a good price but you may even make a new friend.

Why not practise your haggling technique to earn some extra money? Offer to wash your parents' car and see how much money you can get for it. Simply follow these rules:

1. Ask for more than you really want. For example, when they offer you £3, ask for £6 even though you really only want £5. This way you can settle for the price you want.

2. Point out how dirty the car is and how much it needs your services.

3. Convince them the price you offered is excellent value by pointing out how much it costs at the local car wash.

4. Stay calm, be polite and never lose your temper.

HOW TO BE A HORSE WHISPERER

You watch from behind a tree as the muscular 500 kilogram beast thrashes and leaps angrily into the air. Your heart misses a beat as a man strolls calmly towards the horse. Within half an hour, this wild beast and the man have become the best of friends. What you have witnessed is one of the strangest skills known to man … the art of the 'horse whisperer'.

Horse whisperers are people who communicate with horses using body language. It is an essential skill to have if you need to tame a wild horse to ride when on an expedition. Here are some great tips on how to make friends with a wild or angry horse – it may even offer you a ride home.

TRUSTY TECHNIQUES

1. Horses are 'herd' animals, which means they don't like to be on their own. To build a bond with the horse, you need to convince it that you are a herd leader. Stand still and encourage the horse to walk around you in a circle by moving your arms up and down – doing this will keep the horse at a distance from you.

2. Keep eye contact with it at all times. If the horse starts to become angry or frightened, stop moving your arms about. When it calms down, start moving your arms again.

3. When the horse lowers its head and slows its pace, these are signs that it's ready to follow you. Drop your arms down to your sides and allow it to approach.

4. Once the horse begins to follow you around, turn your back to it and start walking in the opposite direction. If the horse still follows you, it is beginning to trust you.

5. Read horse body language. When a horse flattens its ears back and shows the white part of its eyes, this means it is very angry. When a horse's ears are pointed forwards, it is in a friendly mood. Once your horse trusts you, it should start to give you friendly signals.

6. Once you have tamed a horse, it will follow you anywhere. Continue to show it kindness by offering it food – it will be your friendly companion for life.

WARNING. Horse whisperers who work with angry or wild horses have many years' experience. Never approach an upset horse on your own – you may get hurt.

HOW TO BE A 21ST-CENTURY KNIGHT

In days of old, there were no policemen to arrest evil-doers or capture dragons. All the people had to protect them were a brave band of warriors known as knights. There was, however, far more to being a knight than riding into battle.

A knight's training lasted for many years. It started at the age of seven, when a boy of 'noble birth' (from a wealthy or aristocratic family) became what was called a page. Seven years later, he became a squire (a knight's servant), and seven years after that, he eventually became a knight.

After all this training, a knight was expected to be chivalrous (which means kind to others, especially to girls), honest, adventurous, generous, humble (not proud), courteous (good mannered) and courageous (brave). If you think you have the qualities to be a knight in the 21st century, turn the page to take the test.

ARE YOU A MODERN KNIGHT?

Answer **a** or **b** to the questions below to find out.

1. **Chivalry test.** Your sister falls face-first in a puddle. Which do you do?

   a. Help her up.
   b. Laugh.

2. **Bravery test.** You forgot to do your homework. Which do you do?

   a. Bravely admit the truth to your teacher.
   b. Tell the teacher you wanted to do it but couldn't because you were kidnapped by aliens.

3. **Adventurous test.** It's Saturday morning. Would you rather:

   a. Go off on an adventurous quest?
   b. Have a bacon sandwich and watch telly?

4. **Generosity test.** You have one sweet left when your friend tells you he is hungry. Do you:

   a. Give it to him?
   b. Eat it when he is not looking?

5. **Noble birth test.** Does your dad wear:

   a. A crown and robes?
   b. A T-shirt and jeans?

6. Humble test. You score a goal in a school football match. Do you:

a. Turn and applaud the person who passed the ball to you?

b. Pull your shirt over your head, raise your arms and run around the pitch cheering?

7. Courtesy test. You finish eating your lunch. Do you:

a. Thank the person who made it for a lovely meal?

b. Belch and say, 'What's for pudding?'

8. Courage test. Your mum has asked you to tidy your room. Do you:

a. Fearlessly enter the rubbish-strewn room and bravely tackle the mess?

b. Offer to pay your younger sibling to do it for you?

Now add up how many times you answered **a**.

• If you scored between 6 and 8, you are the perfect example of the modern knight. Well done, brave one!

• If you scored 4 or 5, you have knightly qualities in your heart but you need to try harder before you do knightly deeds all the time.

• If you scored less than 4 you are not a knight, but with a lot of hard work, you could prove yourself to be. Go on more adventures and learn more knightly qualities immediately.

HOW TO HANDLE A MEAT-EATING PLANT

A carnivore lives by eating meat. We usually think of animals such as tigers and wolves when talking about carnivores, but one of the most amazing carnivores is a Venus flytrap. Within seconds of an insect landing on this attractive plant, its leaves snap shut. The plant then releases chemical juices which, over a few days, dissolve the creature – slowly eating it alive.

MONSTER MEAT-EATERS

The world of plants may look beautiful and peaceful, but nature is full of different types of meat-eating plants, with many different ways for poor little bugs to meet their doom.

Pitchers. These plants have folded leaves which hold pools of digestive juices for insects to fall into (digestive juices dissolve the insect so the plant can consume it).

Butterworts. These plants have sticky leaves. When a small insect lands on the leaf, it is trapped and covered in digestive juices.

Bladderworts. These plants float on water. Their leaves are shaped like small bags. When a small water creature, such as a water flea, swims into one of the bags, a trapdoor springs shut, trapping it inside.

Corkscrews. These plants have small openings along their roots which attract tiny creatures. Fine hairs across these openings stop them from escaping.

GROW YOUR OWN MEAT-EATING PLANT

Venus flytraps grow in the wild in certain parts of the USA, but they are quite easy to grow yourself. Here's how:

1. Ask your parents to order a bulb from a supplier. (You'll find info about this online.)

2. Venus flytraps need a lot of air to grow, so plant it in a large bowl. Press the bulb into the soil, so that the top of the bulb is level with the top of the soil.

3. Put it on a sunny windowsill. In the winter, cover it with a cloth at night to keep it warm. Water your plant regularly.

4. Feed your plant live bugs, such as worms or insects. The Venus flytrap uses a 'snap trap' which means its leaves snap shut on its prey. Hold the bug with a pair of tweezers inside an open trap, so that it is touching the short hairs on the leaves. Wait until the trap snaps shut. When the trap reopens a few days later, it is ready for you to feed it again.

WARNING. Don't touch the leaves of a Venus flytrap without offering it food. This will fool your plant into snapping its leaves shut, causing it to waste energy, which will shorten its life.

HOW TO MAKE A MEDIEVAL TORCH

If you find yourself exploring a medieval castle on your adventures, you'll probably come across flaming torches made of moulded iron. Generally fixed to banqueting hall walls, they can be removed when you need to explore dark corridors.

TORCH TECHNIQUE

Here's how to make your own medieval-style torch to keep on your bedroom wall, ready and waiting to take with you to throw some light on an adventure.

You will need:

• a small, battery-powered torch • two sheets of A3-sized black card • sticky tape • a ruler • scissors • red and yellow tissue paper • sticky tack • a pencil

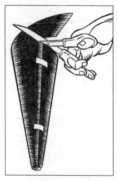

1. Roll one piece of A3 card into a cone shape (like an ice-cream cone) around the battery-powered torch, as shown. Tape the sides together so it stays in shape. Trim the corner from the open end of the cone to leave a circle shape at the top.

Remove the battery-powered torch and put it to one side.

2. Cut strips of red and yellow tissue paper, measuring roughly 10 cm by 2 cm. Tape the ends of each strip to the inside of the cone around the opening – when the battery-powered torch is on, these will look like flames.

3. Out of the second sheet of black card, cut four strips each measuring roughly 10 cm by 4 cm.

4. Stick each strip to the side of the cone around the opening, about 3 cm apart. Curl the top of each strip outward.

5. Cut another strip, roughly 33 cm by 4 cm, from the black card. Tape one end of it to a vertical strip, roughly halfway up the vertical strip's length. Wrap it around all of the vertical strips, then secure the other end with tape, as shown.

6. Cut a strip roughly 20 cm by 10 cm out of the left-over black card. Fix both ends of this strip to your bedroom wall with sticky tack, so that there is a small gap to fit your torch into.

7. Slot your torch carefully into the gap, until it is resting against the wall with the strip holding it in place.

8. Finally, switch on the battery-powered torch and drop it into the open end of the cone so that the light shines out of the top of your medieval torch.

WARNING. Always check with an adult before sticking anything to the wall, as it can leave marks which leave adults grumpy.

HOW TO SURVIVE AN ARCTIC ADVENTURE

Surrounded by dazzling snow as far as the eye can see, you're in the far north of Canada, about to embark on an Arctic adventure. People travelling across the Arctic to the North Pole must walk or ski over hundreds of kilometres of thick ice, and endure terrifying storms and temperatures as low as minus 80°C.

Amazingly, though, people do live in these areas. The Inuit people, who make the Arctic their home, are experts in survival skills. Before you set off across the ice and snow, you spend some time in an Inuit camp learning how to construct shelters out of nothing but snow that will help to keep you safe and warm.

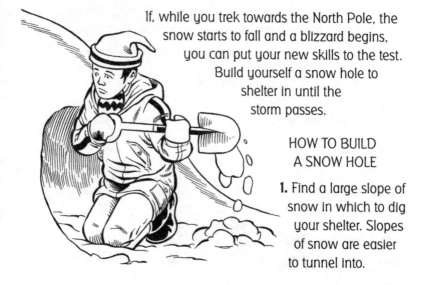

If, while you trek towards the North Pole, the snow starts to fall and a blizzard begins, you can put your new skills to the test. Build yourself a snow hole to shelter in until the storm passes.

HOW TO BUILD A SNOW HOLE

1. Find a large slope of snow in which to dig your shelter. Slopes of snow are easier to tunnel into.

2. Using a shovel, dig a tunnel, about one metre in length, into the side of the slope.

3. Scrape away an area of snow at the end of your tunnel. Continue to scrape out snow until you have made a hole large enough for you to crawl into. Stop scraping when your snow hole is big enough for you to fit yourself and your equipment inside, and tall enough for you to sit up in.

WARNING. Keep the roof of your snow hole as thick as possible – a thick roof will keep your hole warm and also minimize the danger of your snow hole caving in on top of you.

4. Before climbing into your snow hole, spike the ends of your ski poles into the roof. This way, other explorers can spot your shelter and find you easily if they need to.

5. Inside your snow hole, use some of the snow that you scraped away to create a ledge by patting this snow down above the floor of your shelter. Cold air is heavier than warm air and will collect near the floor of your shelter, so having a ledge to sit on will help keep you warm.

6. Put all your belongings in the snow hole, and position something bulky (like your rucksack) in the entrance to keep out some of the cold air.

7. Using a twig or a stick, carefully make three holes in the top of your shelter for ventilation. This way you can safely burn candles inside your snow hole, or light a small camping stove to give you extra warmth.

8. Smooth over the walls and roof inside your snow hole. Your body heat will warm up the snow around you and smoothing the snow on the walls should stop drips.

Now you can shelter from the blizzard in comfort, before heading off on your adventure again.

HOW TO UNDO A GORDIAN KNOT

The famous Greek warrior, Alexander, was one of the greatest soldiers of all time. He was so successful that, over 2,000 years later, he is known by the name Alexander the Great.

Alexander was an ambitious man who wished to rule the whole of Asia. One day he arrived at a city. The people who lived there told him that a man named Gordius had driven a cart into the town over one hundred years before and tied it with a knot so complicated that no one had ever succeeded in untying it. The knot was known as the Gordian Knot, and there was a legend that whoever was able to untie it would one day rule all of Asia.

Alexander tried to untangle it as his troops looked on. Finally, Alexander shouted, 'What does it matter how I loose it?' He then drew his sword and sliced through the knot.

'KNOT' THERE ANY MORE ...

To undo the Gordian Knot, Alexander used what is called 'lateral thinking'. This means, he solved the problem of the knot by looking at it from a different viewpoint – instead of something to untie, he saw it as something to cut through.

Why not use some lateral thinking of your own and amaze your friends by making a knot disappear before their eyes?

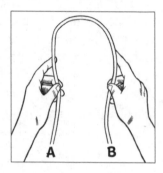

1. Before performing this trick in front of your friends, you need to prepare your magic knot. To do this, hold one end of a piece of string in your right hand (end B) and the other in your left hand (end A).

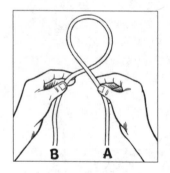

2. Make a loop-shape in the middle of the string by bringing end A over end B.

3. With your right hand, reach through the loop you have made. Grab hold of the middle of string A. Pull it through the loop to make another loop, as shown.

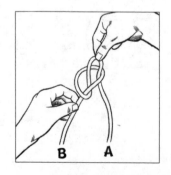

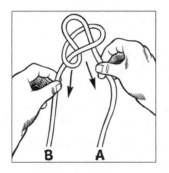

4. Carefully pull down on string A, as shown. This will reduce the size of this second loop. At the same time, pull string B with your other hand, until the second loop is just showing over the first loop that you made.

5. Your string should now look like it has an actual knot in the middle of it.

Be careful not to pull the string on either side of the knot too tight or your magic knot will disappear.

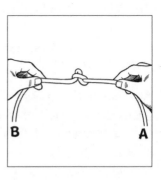

6. Hold the string at either end of the knot and show it to your friends.

Now tell them you are going to magically make the knot disappear.

7. To perform the trick, pass your left hand over the knot and slowly slide it down the string. The knot will untie straightaway. However, to your friends, it will look like you are moving the knot down the string. When your hand gets to the bottom, make a fist and blow on it. Open your hand to show your friends that the knot has disappeared. Voilà!

HOW TO SURVIVE
AN ALIEN ENCOUNTER

Deep in the heart of Nevada, USA, a single, lonely sign stands in the deserted landscape – 'Area 51. No Trespassing.' For years, people have wondered what lies beyond this sign. Area 51 is a US airbase, which is used – so the air force says – to test new top-secret aircraft. The area is a mysterious place because of the strange unexplained lights that appear in the sky above the base.

After a young couple claimed they had been abducted by aliens there in 1961, rumours grew that the air force was testing UFOs (Unidentified Flying Objects) given to the military by aliens. It was said that these spacecrafts were kept in secret, underground bunkers. Some people believe that an alien race called the Reticulians have been watching over the human race for 10,000 years, exchanging their technology with us.

Nobody knows for sure what lies in Area 51 or if humankind has ever had contact with beings from other planets. If you're lucky enough to meet an alien on one of your adventures, stick to the following advice to make sure your encounter is a safe one.

ALIEN ADVICE

• Aliens could look very different from humans, so be prepared to encounter tentacles, many eyes, fangs or slimy bodies. Never look shocked. It is vital that you don't offend an alien. You don't want it to use its laser gun on you! Keep your facial expressions neutral at all times.

• Aliens probably won't speak Earth languages, but they could have a gadget that can help them to translate any language. Make sure you speak slowly and repeat any long words to ensure they understand you.

• If an alien invites you to come on board its spacecraft, politely say no. There are stories about humans being abducted (kidnapped) by aliens, and even though these may not be true, you want to keep your adventures on this planet.

• The alien may be very interested in you, so why not introduce it to some typical Earthling food? Whether you serve afternoon tea or a hamburger and chips, have lots of napkins handy – eating with tentacles is a tricky business, and you don't want the alien to feel embarrassed.

HOW TO SEARCH FOR EL DORADO

For more than 500 years, two words have been whispered around campfires, on the decks of ships, or wherever adventurous people gather – 'El Dorado'. These two words have driven countless explorers to death and madness ... El Dorado means The Golden One and refers to a mythical city on a lake said to be filled with gold and jewels.

THE LEGEND OF EL DORADO

Legend has it, there once was a ruler of an Indian tribe who lived near the modern-day city of Bogotá, the capital of Colombia, South America. After stripping naked and covering his body in mud, this chieftain would pour gold dust over himself and leap into a lake. His tribesmen would then throw gold and jewels into the sacred lake, which remain there to this day ... waiting to be fished out by you.

START A SECRET SEARCH

It might be a few years before you save up the money to travel to South America, but there's nothing to stop you searching for treasure in your local park or jungle in the meantime. Lay a secret trail, that only your friends can follow, which leads to some hidden treasure – a chocolate bar wrapped in gold paper. Here are some real trail signs to kick off your treasure-hunt trail:

A small stone on the right-hand side of a large rock = Turn right.

A small stone on the left-hand side of a large rock = Turn left.

An arrow made from sticks = This way.

Crossed sticks = Not this way.

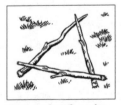

A triangle of sticks = Warning. Danger ahead.

An arrow made of stones above a circle of stones. Walk in the direction of the arrow for as many paces as there are stones inside the circle.

HOW TO DEFEND YOUR BEDROOM FROM INTRUDERS

An adventurer's bedroom is his private kingdom and needs to be defended from intruders – whether they are robbers trying to steal the prized possessions you have brought back from distant lands, interfering brothers and sisters, or nosy parents. It's easy to arrange a few 'surprises' to turn a sneaky visit to your room into a nightmare. Read on to find out how.

A ROOM OF SURPRISES

Stick to it. The first line of defence is your bedroom door. Smear the underneath of the door handle with peanut butter. As soon as the invader grabs the door handle, their hand will be covered in goo.

Scare tactics. Attach a scary mask to some string and hang it at eye-level from the ceiling – use sticky tape to hold it up. The intruder will stare straight into a hideous face as they open your door and be scared out of their wits.

Booby traps. Leave tasty treats out to tempt the intruder into your traps. A bottle of fizzy drink makes a good booby trap if you give it a good shake before leaving it out. As soon as the lid is opened, the greedy thief will be soaked by the drink fizzing up out of the bottle.

Baited biscuits. A cream biscuit makes excellent bait. Separate the two parts of the biscuit, scrape out the cream, and replace it with toothpaste. Put the biscuit back together. No intruder will ever steal your food again!

Tied up in knots. To protect your shelves, all you need is some thin string or fishing line. Tie each object on the shelf to the next one. When an intruder picks something up, everything else will come off as well, making a loud, clattering noise.

Balled over. If you have a cupboard that you don't want people to look in, fill a cardboard box with balls, such as tennis balls, table tennis balls and footballs. Position the box on the top shelf so that the flap falls open when the cupboard opens and balls spill all over the intruder.

Behind the covers. If you suspect a sneaky sibling is borrowing your stuff, arrange some cushions under your duvet cover in the shape of your sleeping body. Pull the cover up high so the cushions are concealed. Hide behind the door. When they open the door, they will think you are tucked up asleep. As they walk in, jump out from behind the door and turn the light on to catch them red-handed.

HOW TO DISCOVER A 'LOST' TRIBE

In the remote forests of New Guinea (a large island north of Australia), many explorers think there are still 'lost' tribes that have had no contact with the outside world. If you want to try and find one yourself, you will need to venture into the island's jungles, where the trees can be so close together that daylight can't get through.

If you do come across a lost tribe on your adventures, remember that the tribe is not really lost – it knows exactly where it is – it is probably you who is lost! If the tribe allows it, spend as much time as you can with them to learn about their culture and their traditions. Read on to improve your chances of a friendly reception.

Be the perfect guest. This is their home not yours, so wait at the edge of the village until they approach you. Offer gifts straightaway so that everybody knows you are not an enemy.

Be respectful. The tribe will not have any of the modern inventions that you are used to, but this does not mean they are primitive. Their culture is as rich and interesting as yours. Always show respect for their way of doing things – never try to teach them to act like you.

Get stuck in. If the tribe allows it, join in and help them with their daily tasks. This may mean going hunting in the jungle, fishing or building living quarters.

Bring your own bed. While trekking through the jungle, you need to be able to build a bed off the ground to sleep in at night. A hammock is best for this, and it's useful too for setting up in a hut if your new friends let you stay the night.

HOW TO MAKE A HAMMOCK BED

Follow the instructions below to find out how to make a hammock bed. Why not practise in a local forest or the park before you set off on your jungle adventure?

You will need:
- an old sheet (a length of old curtain works well, too)
- two long strong ropes • two trees, roughly 2 m apart
- thick fabric (offcuts from an old carpet or mat is ideal)

1. Tie knots in both ends of the sheet, as shown. This is the hammock bed that you will sleep in.

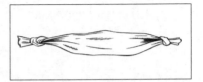

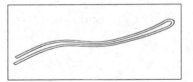

2. Next, you need to hang your hammock bed. To do this, fold one of the ropes double, as shown.

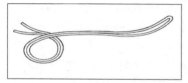

3. Make a loop near the ends of the rope.

4. Thread the ends of the rope through the loop to make a knot.

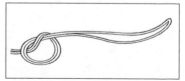

5. Pull the ends of the rope tightly to finish the knot. You should now have a large rope circle, as shown.

WARNING. It's a good idea to tie thick fabric around each tree, roughly a metre up from the base. This will protect the bark of the tree when you tie your rope around it. (See the picture on pages 58 to 59.)

6. Wrap your rope circle around one of the trees, at the point which you tied the thick fabric. Wrap it so that you are holding one loop end (A) in your left hand and the other loop end (B) in your right hand.

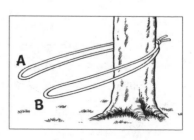

7. Thread loop end A in your left hand through loop end B in your right hand, as shown.

8. You should now have made a new loop. Pull this loop through so that the rope sits tightly on the tree.

9. Make another loop by doubling over the end of this loop as shown.

10. Thread one knotted end of your hammock bed through this loop and pull tightly. One end of your hammock should now be securely fixed to the tree.

11. To secure the other end of your hammock to the second tree, repeat steps **2** to **10** using your other length of rope. Your hammock bed should now hang between the two trees.

WARNING. Never hang a hammock higher than a metre off the ground – this way, if it breaks, you don't have too far to fall.

HOW TO BE A SUPER SWASHBUCKLER

The clash of swords, the swish of blades – there's nothing like the thrill of a sword fight. Of course, in films, the pirates are not really pirates and the battle is a rehearsed 'stunt fight' carried out by actors. To perform your own sword fight with a fellow swordsman, follow this swashbuckling guide:

- The most important part of stunt swordfighting is safety. Only fight with cardboard tubes or foam swords.

- Practice is essential so that each fighter knows exactly what the other person is going to do – this is called 'choreographing' a fight.

- Decide on an order in which you will perform your moves in front of an audience. Then get ready to challenge your friends to a duel and draw your swords!

MASTERFUL MOVES

Master the following moves to create a successful stunt fight.

The thrust attack. Step forwards with your right leg. Punch your right arm out at shoulder height with your sword pointing forwards. At the same time, your opponent must take a step backwards.

The defence parry. To avoid a sword strike, you can do two moves – the parry and the dodge. To practise the parry, ask your opponent to raise his arm and strike downwards at you with his sword.

As his sword comes down on you, put your sword between your body and his sword by placing it horizontally across your body, as shown. His sword will then strike your sword and stop.

The defence dodge. To perform the dodge, ask your opponent to swipe at you with his sword at head height, while you practise dodging the blow by bending both your knees and ducking out of the way.

Adventurous tip. When you practise your routine, remember that sword fighting is all about movement. Move your feet as much as possible while stopping blows with your sword.

The tension builder.
Swordsmen don't spend all their time clashing swords. Build tension by changing the pace of the fight. Walk around in a circle, watching each other and moving your body weight backwards and forwards as if looking for a chance to strike. Try making one or two pretend strikes to unnerve your opponent as you do this.

The dramatic ending. When your opponent strikes and you parry, move in so you are standing very close together, with your swords upwards and crossed. Then push against each other until one swordsman falls to the ground – as if he has been pushed over.

The swordsman still standing then raises his sword above his head and threatens to strike downwards at the swordsman on the floor. The defeated fighter on the ground shouts, 'Mercy!' to end the battle.

Adventurous tip. Although your fight is carefully rehearsed, it needs to look real. Swordfighters battle hard, so there should be lots of shouts, grunts and noisy threats.

HOW TO GET HOME USING NATURE'S CLUES

Whatever adventure you undertake, there is always the danger of getting lost … As the thick fog lifts, you breathe a sigh of relief. You can finally see your surroundings after stumbling around for hours unable to see more than a few metres in front of you. Looking around, you become alarmed at the unfamiliar landscape. You're lost.

All you know is that you pitched your tent somewhere on the north coast of the island, so you have to head north to find your way home. You fumble inside your backpack and pull out your compass only to find it's broken – it must have smashed when you fell down a slippery bank in the fog. You are going to have to use nature to guide you home.

NORTH KNOW-HOW

The easiest way of working out where you are is to use the sun in the sky. If you are in the northern hemisphere (the half of the globe that is above the line of the equator), at 12 noon the sun is due south, and if you are in the southern hemisphere (the half of the globe below the line of the equator), it is due north.

Whichever hemisphere you are lost in, follow these instructions to find north using only a wristwatch:

• To find north in the southern hemisphere, point 12 o'clock on the watch at the sun. Now find the middle point between 12 o'clock and the hour hand. This is north.

• In the northern hemisphere, you'll need to find south first. To do this, point the hour hand at the sun. Find the middle point between the hour hand and 12 o'clock. This is south, so the opposite direction is north.

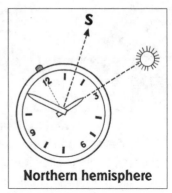

Northern hemisphere

SUNSHINE CLUES

If you don't have a watch, don't worry – you can still work out which way is north by looking around you. Follow these clues to find north and south in the northern hemisphere (the opposite of each clue is true if you are lost in the southern hemisphere).

• Trees can be a useful guide. The side of the tree that faces south will have greater growth, as it will be getting more sunlight. There will be more branches growing horizontally on the southern side, and more branches growing vertically on the northern side.

• The flowers of plants tend to face the sun – south.

• If you are crossing over a hill, the north side will be damper with dew because it gets less sun.

• Keep an eye out for a very tall hill or mountain in the distance. If it has snow on the top, the snow will be thicker and more noticeable on the north side.

• Research has shown that herds of cows tend to stand with their bodies along a north-south line when they are resting or grazing on grass. The direction that their heads are facing is north.

POLE POSITION

Whichever side of the equator you are on, you can use this navigation technique to find north. All you need is a stick and a pebble.

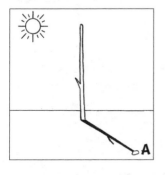

1. Put a long stick in the ground so that it stands upright. The stick will cast a shadow. Put a small pebble (A) at the tip of the shadow.

2. Wait for roughly 20 minutes until another shadow is cast.

3. Place another pebble (B) at the end of the shadow that is now being made by the stick.

4. Next, make a mark midway between pebble A (which is in the west) and pebble B (in the east).

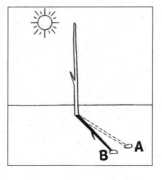

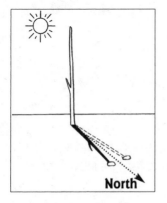

5. The line which runs from the base of your upright stick to the midpoint you have marked is called the north-south line. The direction of this line as it points away from your upright stick shows you which way is north.

HOW TO TAKE ON THE CRESTA RUN

At the first sign of snow, parks are full of people hurtling down hills and banks on their sledges. For an adventurer, though, the one slope that has to be tackled is the Cresta Run in Switzerland.

This is the fastest, most terrifying ride you will ever experience. The toboggan (a type of sledge which has metal runners attached to the underside of a flat board) hurtles down the mountainside in a steep tunnel of ice, going faster and faster over a course that is more than a kilometre long.

A rider lies flat on the toboggan and hangs on desperately while he tears a round steep corners as the course twists and turns down the mountainside. By the time the rider reaches the finish line, he is travelling at more than 125 kilometres per hour.

Since 1885 (when the Cresta Run was first created), the tunnel of ice has been built from scratch every year using fresh snow. The ride has ten corners and the scariest is named the Shuttlecock. This is a steep bank of snow, at which a rider can fall off the run into a huge pile of thick snow. If you fall off here you become a member of the Shuttlecock Club and get a special Shuttlecock tie.

The Cresta Run is only open from December until the end of February, and you have to be over 18 to ride it. If you can't wait until then to ride in the Cresta Run, why not test your tobogganing skills out first on a snowy slope near you? If you don't live in an area which has regular snow fall, you could go to an indoor sledging slope.

Read on, to find out how to set up your own sledging games and see which of your friends will be the champion of the slopes.

LET THE GAMES BEGIN

1. Mark out a course. One competitor must put markers on the hill on the way down (use coats or sticks stuck in the ground). These are your turns and each rider must ride around them on their way down the slope to a line at the end of the course – the finish line.

Adventurous tip. Don't make the turns too wide apart – this will slow the sledge down as you ride.

2. Get into gear. Professional sledgers wear goggles to keep snow out of their eyes, a helmet to protect their heads if they get thrown from their sledge, and thick clothes and gloves to protect them from getting bumps and scrapes and to stop them getting frostbite – a medical condition caused by extreme cold.

3. Carry out safety checks. Each competitor must check their sledge is working properly and there are no loose screws anywhere – a faulty sledge will fall apart when it is ridden.

4. Competitors must sit on their sledges at the top of the slope, facing forwards and sitting upright.

WARNING. Unless you are a Cresta Run entrant, never sledge head first as this can be extremely dangerous.

5. Take it in turns to be the race marshall. The marshall should stand at the bottom of the hill with a stopwatch. He then raises his arm and shouts, 'Ready, Steady, Go!' bringing his arm down on, 'Go!' and times the descent to the finish line.

6. Take it in turns to ride your sledges down the slope to the finish line. If your sledges don't have steering controls, you will have to lean your body to the left or to the right to make the sledge turn. Touch your foot lightly against the snow to slow your sledge and help turn it in the direction you need.

7. Keep a record of how long each competitor takes to complete the course. Each rider has two attempts, and whoever gets to the finish line in the quickest time is the winner.

HOW TO ESCAPE A CAPSIZING SHIP

Anxious to return home after your adventures, you decide to hitch a ride with a merchant ship sailing through the rough seas of the North Atlantic. It is a stormy night, but you feel safe because the ship is a large 16,000-tonne vessel with the latest radar and navigation systems.

As the dark, winter night continues, however, the waves grow larger and the ship begins to rock dangerously. You know that a big enough wave can cause even large ships to capsize, making them tip over and crash into the sea.

Sure enough, a huge wave hits the ship. Water floods the decks. The captain gives the order, 'Abandon ship!' Follow the instructions on the next page to maximize your chances of survival at sea.

Put on your life jacket. A life jacket will keep you afloat in the water without any effort – this will save your body's energy which can be used to keep you warm instead. Try and cover up as much of your bare skin as possible before you put on your life jacket – this will help keep you warmer for longer. If you don't have a life jacket, all is not lost. Your clothes will fill up with pockets of air, which will help to keep you floating, and also stop you from freezing.

Calmly move to the ship's assembly point. The assembly point is an area of the ship where passengers must gather in an emergency. (When boarding a ship, always look to see where this area is.) Do not push or run – this will only increase the panic levels and possibly cause injury among your fellow passengers.

Wait for the life rafts to be released. Wait for your turn to descend. You will be hooked to a life line which descends over the open sea to the raft. Don't be tempted to jump into the sea without waiting for the life line – you might get swept away.

Row, row, row. Once everyone is in the life rafts, the lines holding them to the ship will be cut. Everyone on board will need to row as hard as they can to get away from the ship. Remember, until you are clear, the ship could capsize on top of you at any moment or suck you under the water.

NO LIFE RAFTS

If there are no life rafts, throw something that will float into the water so that you can use it as a point to aim towards when you jump. If your life jacket is inflatable, wait until you leave the ship to inflate it, as you could cause yourself serious injury when you hit the water.

Swim as far away from the ship as possible and steer clear of any oil that might be leaking from the boat – it might catch fire. Swim slowly to keep your energy levels up.

FLOAT FOR YOUR LIFE

If you are stranded in the sea waiting for the rescue boats to arrive, you will need to keep your energy up by using the floating survival technique below:

1. Stop swimming and let yourself float upright in the water.

2. Take a deep breath in, and put your face in the water. Bring your arms up in front of you, but don't lift them out of the water.

Close your eyes and relax in this position, holding your breath for as long as you can comfortably.

3. When you need to breathe again, lift your head up out of the water. Kick your legs as you breathe out to keep you floating. Take a few shallow breaths (smaller breaths) and then repeat steps **2** and **3**.

HOW TO CIRCUMNAVIGATE THE GLOBE

Travelling around the world is one of the greatest adventures of all. To circumnavigate the globe, you must travel through two points on opposite sides of the planet (such as Hamilton in New Zealand and Cordoba in Spain) and arrive back where you started. As these are the only rules, you can choose whatever route and method of transport you wish.

In 2007, Jason Lewis became the first man to successfully circumnavigate the globe using only muscle power. He cycled, hiked, swam, rowed, sailed, pedaloed and kayaked. He even roller-bladed across the USA during an amazing 74,000 kilometre trip that took him across oceans, deserts, jungles and mountains.

The two points on the opposite sides of the globe that Jason travelled through were a point in the Atlantic Ocean and a point in Australia (marked as crosses below). His whole route is marked on this map.

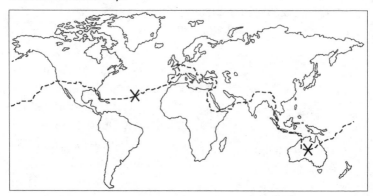

It took Jason 13 years. His boat capsized, he suffered blood poisoning, broke both legs, and was attacked by a giant crocodile and Sumatran bandits, before arriving back in London, where he had started.

Many courageous adventurers have tried to be even speedier than Jason by plotting a route around the world that takes them across a short stretch of sea that connects Alaska and Russia, called the Bering Strait.

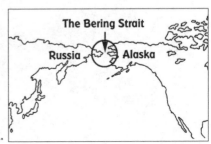

Having done your research, you're now ready to begin your globe-crossing adventure. You decide to go for a route that takes you across America to Alaska, where you will tackle the Bering Strait. Good luck!

CROSSING THE BERING STRAIT

In winter, this treacherous channel of water is clogged with large slabs of drifting ice, so sailing across is impossible. You must get across using a combination of walking and, if necessary, swimming. With your tent, sleeping bag, ice axe and other provisions safely stowed on a sledge, and with your drysuit on to stop the freezing water making contact with your skin, you begin to cross the stretch of ice.

THINGS TO 'BERING' MIND

• Aim for the largest, flattest, most stationary pieces of ice to walk on. Be aware of melting ice. Screeching or creaking sounds are tell-tale signs that the ice isn't secure enough to take your weight.

• Strong currents in the water cause smaller channels of water that break the ice – these are called 'leads'. If an unexpected lead opens up, jump straight in and swim, pulling your sledge behind you. When you reach the next chunk of ice, use your ice axe to pull yourself up and out of the water. Spend as little time as possible in the water to stop your body temperature from dropping too low.

• Never travel when it is too dark to see. When night falls, pitch your tent on the biggest piece of ice you can find, but be prepared for your ice island to drift slightly off course during the night.

Once you've successfully crossed the Bering Strait, give yourself a quick pat on the back and crack on with your circumnavigation of the globe.

Adventurous tip. To make your trip as fast as possible, try to get permission from the Russian authorities to allow you entrance into Russia before you cross the Bering Strait. Otherwise you risk being caught by the Russian police – there's nothing like getting arrested to hold up an adventure!

HOW TO GET OUT OF BEING TIED UP

You're sitting in a smelly, damp room looking down at the thick rope binding your wrists. The guard checks the knots he has just tied and leaves the room, slamming the door behind him.

You've travelled thousands of kilometres with the key to a secret language that will unlock the door of an ancient Egyptian tomb filled with treasure.

The key is sewn into a secret pocket of your coat-lining. A few metres from your destination, a greedy tomb raider captures you. Once you are searched, they will find the key and steal the treasure that is hidden in the tomb.

As soon as the guard leaves you alone, as if by magic, you slip your hands easily out of the rope. Suddenly, you hear footsteps. You quickly slip your hands back into the knots. Seconds later the door opens and the guard reappears. Coming over, he checks the knots once more, then grins and leaves.

With the guard out of sight, your hands are free again. You open a window, drop to the ground and run as fast as you can to the hidden tomb. Your secret key is safe.

ESCAPE TACTICS

All adventurers run the risk of capture. There is, however, a secret method to help you escape. If your enemy is tying you up, he will be nervous that you will break free until you are tightly bound. This means you can control his movements.

To practise this escape tactic, find a piece of string and ask a friend to play the role of the enemy. Follow these instructions to learn how to escape from knots:

1. Put your left arm out so that the palm of your hand is facing upwards. Wrap the string once around and lay the string over the inside part of your wrist, as shown.

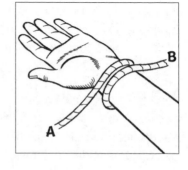

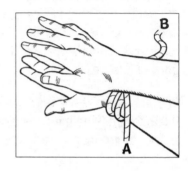

2. Wrap the string around your wrist again so it makes an X-shape, as shown.

3. Put your right wrist next to your left wrist.

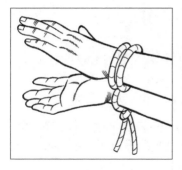

4. Flip both your wrists over, so that the string goes over your right wrist, as shown.

Ask your friend to tie a tight knot in the string so your wrists are tied together.

5. To escape, twist your right wrist round and the string will open up so that you can easily slip your hands out.

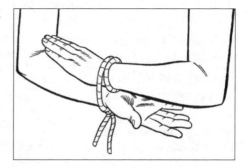

Adventurous tip. Once you have mastered how to escape from knots, perform this trick in front of an audience. It is really impressive if your audience can't see how you escape.

To do this, sit down at a table after you have been tied up, with your wrists out of sight. Now slip your hands out. For the finale of the trick, bring them up above the table. Your friends should gasp in amazement at your escapology skills.

HOW TO RIDE WHITEWATER RAPIDS

You've teamed up with four other brave souls for a river-rafting adventure. So far, everything has been very peaceful. The river is calm, and so are you as you paddle smoothly along.

Things are about to change. As you approach a bend, the most experienced rafter among you tells you that the rapids are about to begin. You can hear the water crashing around rocks and thundering downhill. Suddenly you feel very glad that you are wearing a life jacket and more importantly a helmet – this water is about to get wild!

RIDE THOSE RAPIDS

The rider with the most experience is seated at the back of the large rubber boat. He uses his paddle as a rudder to steer the boat through the rapids, avoiding obstacles in the water. It's up to you and the other three rafters to paddle with all your might and keep your boat moving along the safest course.

Suddenly, the right-hand side of the boat rises and is about to flip over. Your team quickly moves to the right-hand side of the boat so that the weight lowers it down. With the boat level,

you all paddle furiously to dodge the rocks while watching for overhanging branches that could knock you out of the boat.

Eventually, the crashing water stops and you are once again drifting slowly on calm water. Congratulations. You have ridden whitewater rapids and lived to tell the tale.

RAPID-RIDING RULES

To ride whitewater rapids to safety, follow these essential
rapid-riding rules:

- Teamwork is very important. If you don't work together,
your boat will tip over and you will end up in the water.
Pay attention to your leader's instructions at all times.

- Keep a firm grip on your paddle. Keep one hand over the
top of the paddle (called the T-grip) for extra control. This will
also make sure you don't whack your fellow riders on the
head with your paddle as you stroke through the water.

- Don't sit straight and rigid in the boat. By relaxing your
posture and letting your body move with the boat, you're
more likely to stay in your seat for the whole ride.

- Try and steer the boat towards patches of calmer water,
called 'eddies'. These are formed when the water swirls
behind large obstacles in the river, like rocks or logs, and
will help you to get your breath back before you tackle the
next big drop.

- If you find yourself going for an unexpected swim, don't
panic and don't let go of your paddle. Try to swim back to
the boat so that the others can pull you back in.

- If the water is flowing too fast and you can't swim against
it, lie on your back and float down the river feet-first until
the boat catches up with you.

WARNING. Riding rapids is extremely dangerous and not
something you do by yourself. However, there are organized
whitewater rafting trips where you can enjoy the experience
in safety.

HOW TO TELL A CRACKLING CAMPFIRE TALE

The boys sit huddled around the crackling campfire, listening to the hoots of owls and the rustling of animals in the dark woods surrounding them. You break the silence:

'Did I ever tell you about the famous legend of El Dorado?'

The boys look at you, shaking their heads and waiting to hear all about your adventure in search of the lost city of El Dorado (see pages 80 to 81 to read all about this legend).

All adventurers have tales to tell, but just because something exciting happened to you doesn't mean it will fascinate your audience when you recount the tale. Every adventurer needs to be able to tell stories that will hold their listeners' interest. Read on to learn how to tell a tale that will keep your listeners hanging on every single word.

STORYTELLING SKILLS

• First, think of a story to tell. It might be an adventure you have had, or something you have heard about or read. The story should suit the situation – campfire tales are told outside in the dark, so ghost stories or adventures are good.

• Make sure you know the story very well. There's nothing worse than stopping while you try to remember what happens next. You need to keep your listeners absorbed.

• The story needs to be fairly simple. If there are too many characters and too many different things happening at the same time, people will become confused and lose interest.

• Think of a way to make the start of the story as interesting as possible. You want to grab your audience's attention straightaway. Practise the end of the tale as well, as this is the most important part.

• Use your voice to bring the story to life. Don't say everything in the same way or people will get bored. You could speak quietly when talking about something ghostly, speed up at the exciting parts, or pause to create tension.

• You can also use your body to add to the drama. For example, you could mimic the actions of the characters by throwing your hands in front of your face in shock at certain points in the story.

• When you are describing events, picture them in your mind. Things are always easier to describe and more real to the listeners if you can picture the scene as you describe it.

• Don't rush the story. If you enjoy the telling of the tale, then your listeners will enjoy listening to it.

HOW TO DODGE POISONOUS DARTS

One of the deadliest weapons in the world is the poisonous dart. Tribesmen in remote areas know every plant in their jungle – which can be eaten, which can heal and which can kill. Using this knowledge, they dip darts into the juice of poisonous plants, making them so deadly that one puncture is enough to kill a man. Some tribes even collect poison from poisonous frogs to wipe their darts with.

The dart is fired from a blowpipe. This is a hollow, wooden pipe up to two metres long. The tribesman silently stalks his prey through the jungle and, when he has a clear view, raises the pipe to his lips. Taking careful aim, he blows quickly, shooting the dart towards the target at great speed. The dart strikes and the poison quickly spreads through the victim's body.

DART-DODGING TECHNIQUE

If you find yourself being stalked by hunters with poisonous darts during an expedition through the jungle, there are two things to remember which could save your life:

1. Blowpipes are very accurate, and skilled hunters can hit their target from some distance. Stay in dense bushes so the hunter cannot get a clear shot at you. Because the blowpipe is two metres long, it is more difficult to use if there is lots of foliage around.

2. Poisonous darts can reach speeds of over 28 metres per second. By the time the hunter fires, it is too late for you to dodge the dart. Keep a careful lookout in the trees on either side of your path so that you spot the attacker first.

Good dodging is about being aware of what is going on around you and reacting quickly. If you want to practise your dodging skills, there's nothing better than a game of Dodge Ball.

HOW TO PLAY DODGE BALL

1. You will need at least six players to play Dodge Ball, plus a referee with a whistle. You need as many light foam balls as you have players.

2. Mark out a court on some grass. To do this, lay string on the ground to make a rectangular-shaped court that is 18 metres long and 9 metres wide. The lines at opposite ends of the court are called the 'base lines'. Next, mark a line on the ground along the middle. This is your 'centre line'. Finally, mark two lines on the ground across the width of the court, 2.5 metres either side of the centre line. These are called your 'attack lines'.

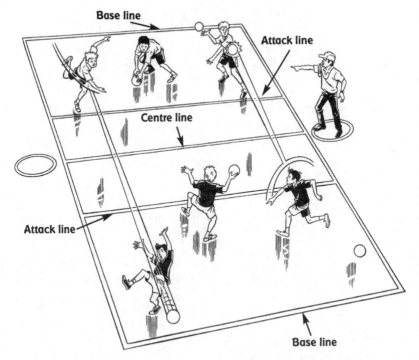

Base line

Attack line

Centre line

Attack line

Base line

3. Put all the balls on the centre line and split into two teams. Each team member must line up along the base line at either end of the court. The referee then blows a whistle to begin the game.

4. Each player must now run to pick up a ball from the centre line. Standing behind their attack lines, players must then throw balls at the other team, trying to hit a part of their body below the head. At the same time, each player must try and dodge out of the way of balls being fired at them by their opposing team.

5. If a player is hit, he must leave the court. When one team has no players left on the court, the other team has won.

HOW TO ESCAPE FROM THE BELLY OF A WHALE

You might think being chewed into pieces by a great white shark is the worst thing that could happen to you at sea, but what if a whale swallowed you whole and left you sitting in its stomach?

There are many stories of people being swallowed by whales throughout history. In the Bible there is a tale of Jonah, who disobeys God and is swallowed by a whale as punishment. In the story about Pinocchio, the wooden puppet is swallowed up by a whale, but he lights a fire in the whale's stomach and the whale sneezes him out to freedom!

Although scientists agree that the mouths and bellies of some whales are big enough to swallow a human whole, it is very unlikely that you will ever find yourself inside one. This is because whales like to eat sea creatures, not humans. Some don't even have teeth, but filter out tiny animals such as krill through comb-like structures in their mouths called 'baleen'.

Toothed whales eat fish, squid and octopus, and some even tackle penguins, seals and walruses ... but rarely humans.

If a whale does accidentally confuse you with his supper and swallow you up, don't panic. There is plenty of room – a whale's stomach can hold nearly a tonne of fish – and hopefully enough oxygen to breathe. It will feel very hot because a whale's belly is surrounded by thick 'blubber' (fat) which keeps it warm in cold seas, but resist the temptation to take off all your clothes – the whale's digestive juices will react with your skin as it tries to digest you. Keep as much of your skin covered as possible and don't touch anything.

To avoid starving to death, try tickling the stomach or jumping up and down to give it a tummy ache to make it sick – you would then come out with the sick ... nice! Making it sneeze like Pinocchio won't work in the real world as whales sneeze through their blow holes and you would get stuck. If none of this works, as a last resort use a large knife to try to cut through the thick stomach wall to freedom. Whichever way you try and escape from the belly of the whale, it won't be a pleasant experience ...

HOW BIG IS BIG?

The biggest animal alive on Earth today is the blue whale. It can grow up to 34 metres long and weighs over 120 tonnes. Its tongue alone weighs 4 tonnes. To imagine just how big this is put a stick in the ground. Walk 46 steps. If you were standing by a blue whale's mouth, its tail would be back where the stick is pointing out of the ground. Avoid swimming in front of a whale's mouth at all times, and you should be safe.

HOW TO EXPLORE A MUMMY'S TOMB

The Valley of the Kings, in the west of Egypt, is a hostile place where the fierce African sun has turned the valley into a dry, barren landscape. However, the most amazing treasures have been found underground ... the riches of the ancient Egyptian pharaohs.

After death, the bodies of these rulers were turned into mummies – which means they were specially preserved so that they didn't rot – and placed in tombs surrounded by the treasures that they collected in their lifetime.

The more famous tombs are in huge pyramids further north. These pyramids were easy for tomb robbers to see, so all the treasures have already been stolen from them. However, in secret, underground tombs in the Valley of the Kings, gold and jewels may still be found.

TOMBING TACTICS

To discover an unexplored tomb, follow the advice below.

Take a torch and a rope. Tombs often have twisting passageways, blind alleys and many chambers. It is a good idea to tie some rope at the entrance to an opening where you suspect a tomb to be. Start unwinding it as you go in. To find your way out again, you'll need to follow the rope back to the entrance – just like Theseus did when he entered the maze to kill the Minotaur (see pages 21 to 23).

Take small steps. If you are lucky enough to have discovered a tomb, move around carefully. You do not know what steps the builders of tombs took to protect the pharaoh. There may be deep holes waiting to swallow unsuspecting explorers or trap doors that suddenly close the exit route, leaving you to die of thirst in the darkness.

Wear gloves. Always wear gloves in case there is poison smeared over the treasure to stop tomb robbers.

Be curse aware. Many of the pharaohs cursed their tombs to stop tomb raiders. If you find a tomb that is cursed, turn to pages 120 to 123 to learn how to decode an encrypted curse and escape a fate worse than death.

Take a trusty team. Only go tomb hunting with people you trust. A tomb full of unclaimed treasure does strange things to people and you don't want anyone trapping you in the tomb and making off with all the gold.

Report your findings. If you do discover a tomb filled with ancient treasures, report it to the local museum immediately. These new findings will help archaeologists (people who study remains from the past) to learn more about the ancient Egyptians.

WARNING. It is illegal to take treasure out of the country that you discovered it in. If you do discover an ancient Egyptian tomb, tell the local authorities immediately and never take any treasure for yourself.

TAKE THE MUMMY TEST

Before you set off on your expedition, it's a good idea to learn as much as you can about Egyptian mummies and their tombs in case you come face to face with one.

Answer TRUE or FALSE for each statement below.

1. To turn a pharaoh's body into a mummy, the insides were taken out and the body stuffed with linen or sawdust.

2. The internal organs of a dead pharaoh – such as the liver, stomach and lungs – were put in jars and stored inside the tomb.

3. The brains of pharaohs were removed by pulling them out through the nose.

4. The ancient Egyptians did not just make human mummies. Thousands of cat mummies have been discovered … even a mummified hippopotamus.

5. Some mummies had their eyes replaced with onions.

6. Food was left in tombs in case mummies got hungry.

7. The mummified bodies of men and women were dyed different colours to help tell them apart. Men were painted red, and women were painted yellow.

8. Milk and wine were sometimes rubbed into the skin of the mummies during the mummification process to act as moisturizers.

9. People once ground mummies into powder to use as medicine.

10. The biggest mummy ever found weighed nearly two tonnes and was called Two-tonne-kamun.

Answers. Believe it or not, all the statements are true, except for the last one, which is just silly!

HOW TO ESCAPE THE CURSE OF A PHARAOH

If you've discovered the tomb of an ancient Egyptian pharaoh while digging in the deserts of Egypt (see pages 116 to 119 to learn how to explore a mummy's tomb), be warned that the pharaoh buried there might have left a curse for whoever disturbs his rest …

THE CURSE OF TUTANKHAMUN

All explorers shudder at the tale of one of the greatest archaeological discoveries of all – when, in 1923, Howard Carter and his team broke into the burial chamber of Tutankhamun. Rumour has it, no one noticed the hieroglyphs (ancient Egyptian writing) on the wall of the chamber. Translated, the hieroglyphs said:

> *Death will come to those who disturb the sleep of the pharaohs.*

It is said that within two months, the first member of the team was dead – killed by an infected mosquito bite. Shortly afterwards, another team member mysteriously fell into a coma and died. A third died soon after returning to England, and so the tragedy continued. Within a few years more of the men that had made the discovery had died. The leader of the team, Howard Carter, however, lived to old age. Whether you believe in curses or not, you don't want to wait for the revenge of the pharaoh to strike you down.

A CURSED DISCOVERY

Imagine you get the chance to see an ancient Egyptian tomb with your own eyes. Suddenly, you find yourself falling into an underground chamber. You hit the ground hard. Looking up, you see the hole far above. There's no way you can get back up! Finding your torch in your pocket, you switch it on. Scanning the chamber, you see an ancient wall with hieroglyphic writing on it. Using your hieroglyphic translator you read on to discover your fate:

Only he who is wise enough to solve the Pharaohs' riddle shall pass. All others will be struck down dead by the Pharaohs' protectors.

Below this, you spot a piece of old parchment (on the next page). Read on to discover how to escape the curse.

Place the three symbols below in the correct order and a door will open to riches beyond your dreams. Fail, and you will suffer a fate worse than death.

All three of the symbols in Row 1 are the right ones, but they are all in the wrong place.

Row 1:

Each row below is a clue to the correct order. Each contains one of the three correct symbols, but still in the wrong place. Use these clues to work out the correct order of the three symbols above.

Row 2:

Row 3:

Row 4:

Adventurous tip. The way to solve this puzzle is to use what is called a 'process of elimination'.

To do this, look at Row 1. This shows you that the symbol **[]]]** cannot be in position 1.

Row 2 shows you that the symbol **[]]]** cannot be in position 2 either.

This means that symbol **[]]]** has to go in Position 3.

Use the same system to work out where the [≋] symbol and the [⬗] symbol need to go.

So, did you find your way through to the treasure or did you fall victim to the curse? Turn the page upside down to discover if you've beaten the curse and found the gold.

The symbol with the three, thick, vertical lines goes in Position 3.

The owl symbol goes in Position 2.

Answer. The symbol with the three, thin, horizontal lines goes in Position 1.

HOW TO MAKE AN ADVENTURE JOURNAL

All true adventurers know how important it is to keep a journal. This is because they know that people will be fascinated by their exciting experiences and will want to read all about them. Follow the steps below to make your own personalized adventure journal.

You will need:
- a spiral-bound notebook
- a selection of exciting images cut out from magazines (ships, spacecrafts, monsters or places you want to go to are ideal) • PVA glue and a glue brush • white paper • scissors

1. Open the notebook out flat so that you can see both the front and back covers. Place it on a table.

2. Arrange your images on both the front and back covers of the notebook. Once you have decided on the best arrangement, put the images to one side and paint a thin layer of PVA glue over the front and back covers. Place the images on the layer of glue in your preferred arrangement.

3. Add another thin layer of glue and leave your journal overnight to allow the glue to dry completely.

4. Cut a rectangle shape out of the white paper and stick it down on the front of the notebook. Write 'The Amazing Adventures Of [your name here]'.

Adventurous tip. Keep your journal in a sealed plastic freezer bag. This will ensure that it doesn't get wet when you're riding whitewater rapids or wading through rivers.

WRITING YOUR JOURNAL

At the end of each day, find a comfortable rock to sit on and write the date and time on a fresh page in your journal.

Here are some things every adventurer should make a note of in his journal each day:

- Really gross things you had to eat that day.

- Who you met and the friends you made.

- Near-death experiences – how you escaped danger and got away with your life just in time.

- The best and worst things that happened to you that day. This way you get an idea of how you felt about events rather than just what happened.

- The new skills you learnt – for example, how to tie a new knot or how to set up your hammock. If you learnt how to say hello in a new language, jot it down in your journal.

HOW TO PUBLISH YOUR ADVENTURES

You've solved riddles, discovered lost tribes, explored tombs, dived to the bottom of the ocean, tackled killer snakes, tamed wild horses and ridden the rapids. All that's left to do now is to tell everyone about your wonderful adventures!

Read on to learn how to publish your adventures so that your friends and family can read all about them. You can type your adventures out on a computer or write them out by hand.

1. Write an exciting introduction on the first page that will entice readers to read on, such as, 'Inside are many thrilling adventures, such as diving for treasure, exploring an Egyptian mummy's tomb, fighting terrifying beasts, and hurtling headfirst down steep mountains.'

2. Choose eight of the best adventures and think of a title for each one. It needs to be something that will capture your readers' interest – for example, instead of, 'Looking for Fossils', use a title such as, 'Hunting for Dinosaurs'.

3. Write out what happened on each adventure. Refer to your adventure journal (see pages 124 to 125) to help you remember small details, such as what you ate on your travels.

4. Draw or cut out a picture from a magazine to illustrate each of your adventures. Stick your chosen picture down on the first page of a new chapter.

5. Finally, photocopy as many copies as you need and staple the pages of each publication together to make a booklet. Hand out your published works to friends and family.

HOW TO BE A MODEST ADVENTURE HERO

The greatest challenge faced by any adventure hero is to avoid annoying everybody by boasting about your adventurous exploits and heroic deeds. To do this you will need to master the art of modesty – the opposite of boasting. Read on to learn how you can be a hero and still be liked by everyone.

Mention your adventures in passing. With any luck, your friends will ask you more about them. More importantly, you won't be accused of talking about yourself all the time!

Act like it's not important. If you had a run-in with a wild beast on an adventure, show your friends the scratch. When they ask how you got it, say, 'Oh, just a Komodo dragon.' They will be secretly impressed by how brave you are.

Don't attract attention. Never wear treasures that you found on your travels to school – your friends will think you're a show-off. If you hand them out as gifts, your friends will think you are generous instead.

Thank friends and family. If you are lucky enough to win an award for bravery, or for your contribution to science, thank everyone who helped you do it – including your mum for making your packed lunch!

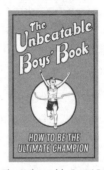